Chess for Kids

Learn to Play Chess in a Fun and Simple Way

Sam Lemons

Learning Through Activities

SPECIAL BONUS!

Want These 2 Books For FREE?

Get **FREE**, unlimited access to these and all of our new kids books by joining our community!

Scan W/ Your Camera To Join!

Welcome
to
Chess for Kids!

LET'S GROW TOGETHER!

We Would Really Appreciate It If You Could Take A Moment To Leave Us A Review On Amazon!

Table of Contents

Introduction

Chess is a game of strategy, where two players battle each other out with the goal being to try and threaten and capture each other's King.

Both players start the game with 16 pieces, one player with a set of black pieces, the other player with a set of white pieces.

Chess is played on a checkered 8x8 board, made of black and white squares.

Chapter 1
Board & Pieces

In this chapter, you are going to learn the basics of chess. First, you'll become more familiar with the board and then meet the pieces one by one.

They're an interesting bunch!

To help you along, you will have a very special guide throughout this book and I can't wait for you to meet him. Let's get started!

Hi! My name is Pawnie and we are going to learn how to play chess together. Are you ready?

But first, what's your name?

My name is ....

Where should we start?

Oh, I know! The chessboard!

Chessboard

The board used to play chess has 8 files and 8 rows (called ranks) with a pattern of black and white squares.

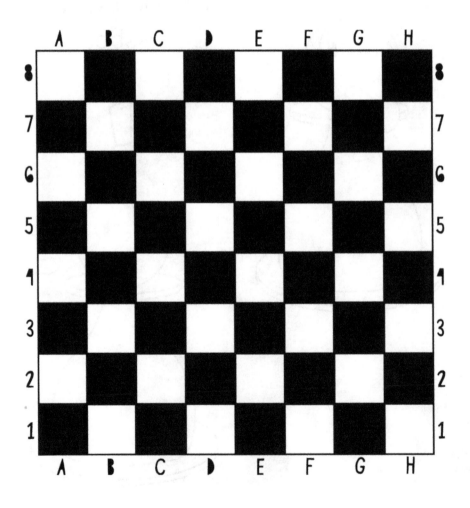

When the board is in the correct position, you will have a black square on your left and a white one on your right.

From the white player's side of the board, each file has an A through to letter H, from left to right, and each rank has a 1 through to number 8, starting from the closest rank.

With these numbers and letters, you can identify each square. For example, the white pieces' black corner is A1 and the white one is H1.

What should we
do next?

Oh, I know! Let's
meet my friends!

Pieces and Their Moves

There are six different pieces in chess: King, Queen, Bishop, Knight, Rook and Pawn. They can be black or white and each player can have as few as just one piece of a certain type, or as many as eight of them.

Now, the fun bit. Unlike some other games, in chess, each piece moves its own way. A little like how a crab moves only sideways, a kangaroo moves by hopping or a snake can only slither. You'll soon learn how each piece moves and their starting positions on the chessboard.

Ready to meet Pawnie's friends?

Hello! I'm the King of this game, which means I can move in whatever direction I want! But, I'm only allowed to move one step at a time.

From now on, black and white Kings will be pictured like this:

Each player has just *one* King. The black player's King is first placed in the E8 white square and the white player's King goes in the E1 black square.

A trick to remembering their position is that the Kings are placed in a square that is the opposite color to that of the piece. So black King will start on a white square, and a white King will start on...? Yes, a black square!

Kings, being the Kings that they are, can move in any direction, but only one step at a time and they can't be in a square that is being attacked by their opponent.

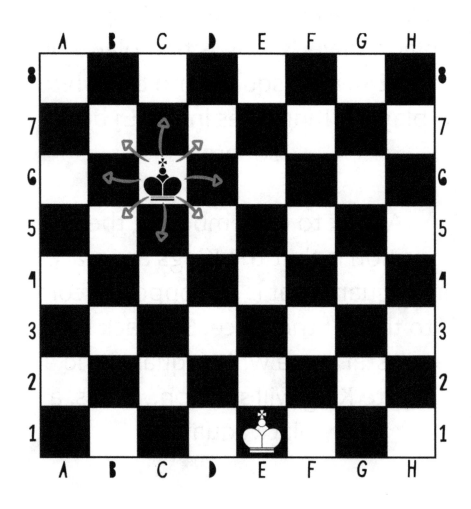

Hi! I'm the Queen and I can move in *any direction* and also in as many steps at the same time. I'm a long-distance piece and I am pretty special because I can do whatever I want! Well, that is except jump.

From now on, black and white Queens will be pictured like this:

Each player has just one Queen. The black player's Queen is first placed in the D8 black square and the white player's Queen goes in the D1 white square, next to her King of course.

It's easy to remember their position knowing that the Queens are placed in a square of the same color as that of the piece.

Queens can move forward, backward, to the left, to the right, or following diagonal paths, as many steps as the player needs.

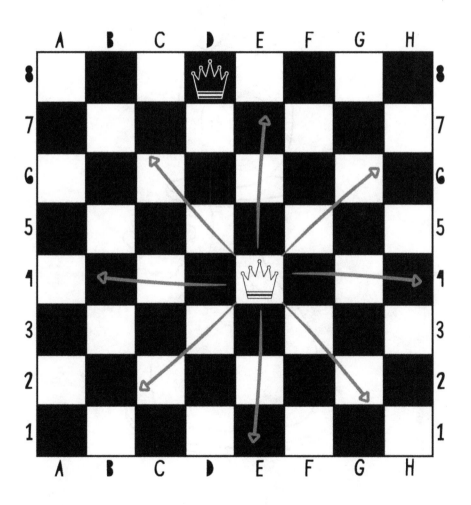

My name is Bishop, nice to meet you!
I can move through the whole
board, but only in diagonal paths.

From now on, black and white
Bishops will be pictured like this:

Each player has two Bishops. The
black player's Bishops are firstly
placed in the C8 and F8 squares and
the white player's Bishops go in the
C1 and F1 squares.

You can remember their position
knowing that one Bishop goes next
to the Queen and the other one goes
next to the King - the best friends of
the King and Queen!

Bishops can move any number of
steps, forward and backward, but
always following diagonal paths.
They can't jump over other pieces.

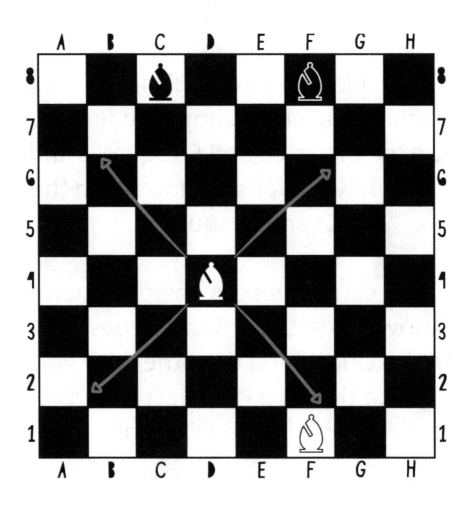

Hello! I'm the Knight and I am the only piece that can jump over other pieces. My moves are a little bit more complicated... but I think - more fun!

From now on, black and white
Knights will be pictured like this:

Each player has two Knights. The
black player's Knights are firstly
placed in the B8 and G8 squares and
the white player's Knights go in the
B1 and G1 squares.

Remember their position by
knowing that, from the center of the
board to the edges, the Knights go
right next to the Bishops. Think of
them as the Bishop's horses to ride.

They can take two steps to the left
or right and then one step forward
or backward.

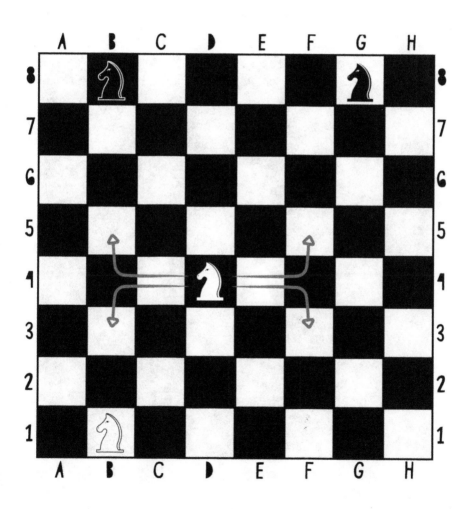

They can also take two steps forward or backward and then one step to the left or right.

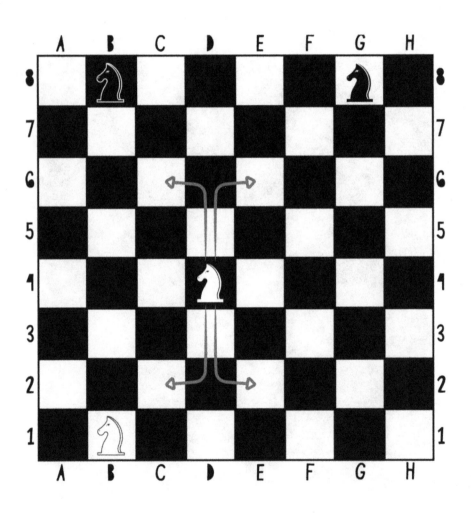

Also, they can take one step to the left or right and then two steps forward or backward.

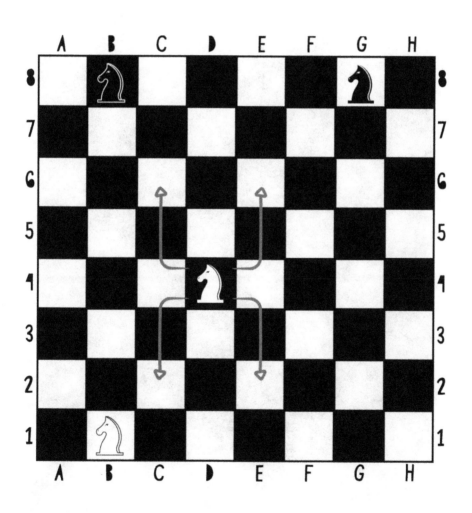

Or they can take one step forward or backward and then two steps to the left or right.

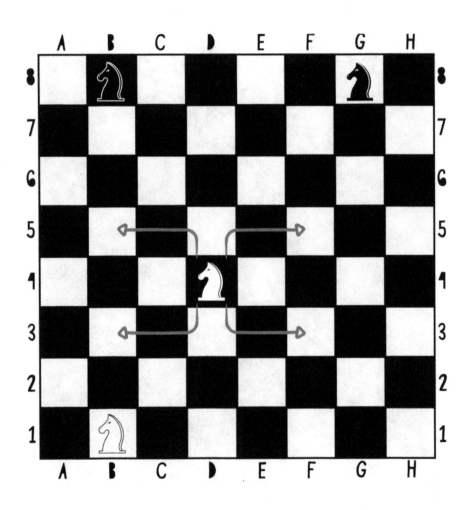

Knights can jump over other pieces and all their moves have the shape of an L or a 3x2 rectangle. All their moves together look like this:

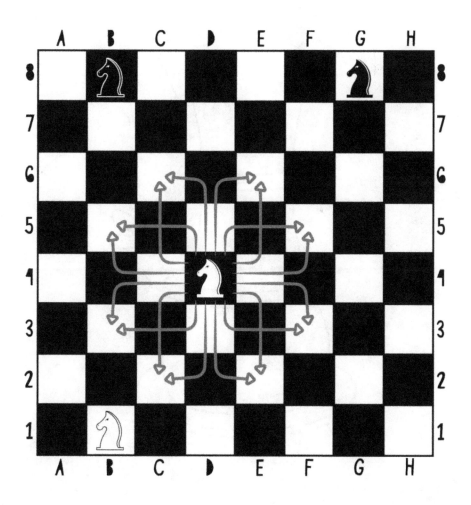

The Rook salutes you! I move back and forth or sideways and I can jump just to protect our King.

From now on, black and white Rooks will be pictured like this:

Each player has two Rooks. The black player's Rooks are firstly placed in the A8 and H8 squares and the white player's Rooks go in the A1 and H1 squares.

It's so easy to remember the Rooks are placed in the corners of the board, right next to the Knights.

Rooks can move forward, backward, to the left or right, any number of steps, basically in a straight line. They can't jump over other pieces, except for 'castling'.

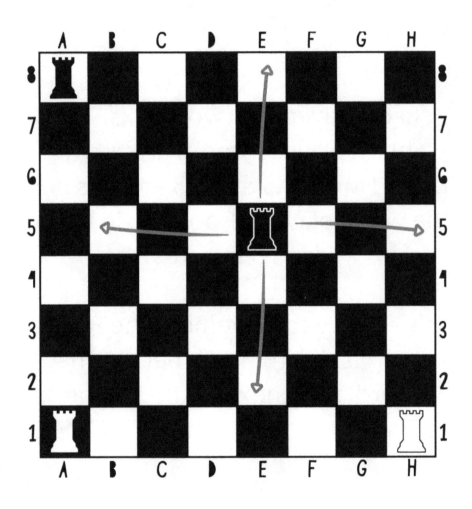

Don't forget about me! I'm a Pawn and I can move just one step ahead, two if it's my first move. I may not be able to do much at once, but I have the ability to become whoever I want: Queen, Rook, Bishop, or Knight!

From now on, black and white Pawns will be pictured like this:

Each player has eight Pawns. The black player's Pawns are firstly placed on the A7 through H7 squares and the white player's Pawns go in the A2 through H2 squares.

It's easier to remember the Pawn's position knowing that there's a Pawn in front of all the other pieces that are already placed on the chessboard.

Pawns can only move one step forward each time, but from their initial position, they can take two steps. They can't jump over other pieces.

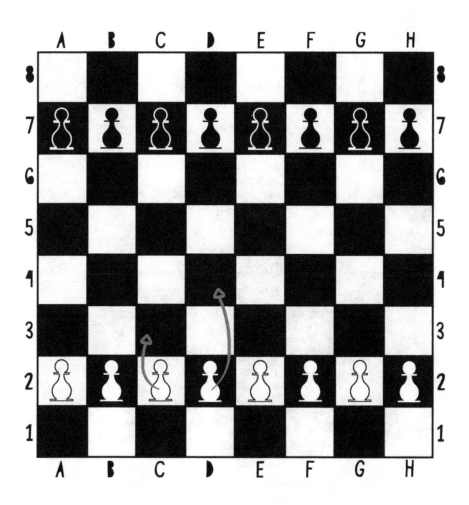

Now that you have met all the pieces, know their positions and how they move, this is how the board looks like at the beginning of the game:

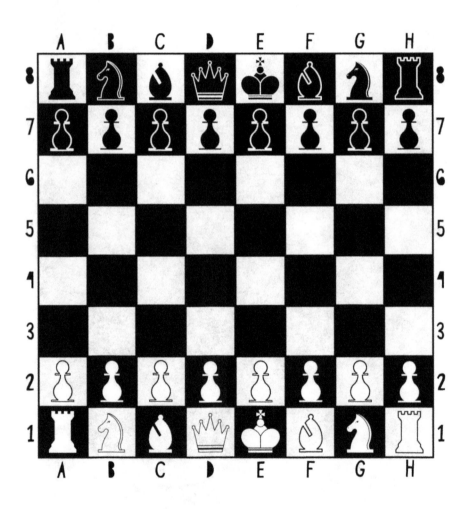

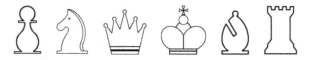

Exercises

Now that you've met all of Pawnie's friends, you've learned a lot of new things. How about a few activities to help you remember everything?

Ready, steady... Go!

Match each piece on the left with its name:

 Knight

 Queen

 Bishop

 Pawn

 Rook

 King

Now, who would say that? Read each sentence carefully and circle the piece who said it:

#1 I can take two steps forward on my first move.

#2 I can move in any direction and as many steps as I want.

#3 I can always jump over other pieces.

#4 I can move in any direction, but taking one step at a time.

#5 I can move back and forth, but just along diagonal paths.

Can you find all the pieces in this word search puzzle? Remember, there are six different pieces.

K	N	I	G	H	T	B
I	J	G	T	S	D	I
R	O	O	K	A	M	S
Q	R	U	I	O	P	H
K	E	A	N	P	A	O
B	S	H	G	Y	W	P
V	Q	U	E	E	N	B

What Would You Do?

In this section there can be one or more than one correct answer and it's up to you to choose it. You can move the pieces as you like and in as many ways as you want.

Have fun!

This board looks a little bit empty. How sad! Let's fill it up. Where would you place the missing Rook, Knight, King and Queen?

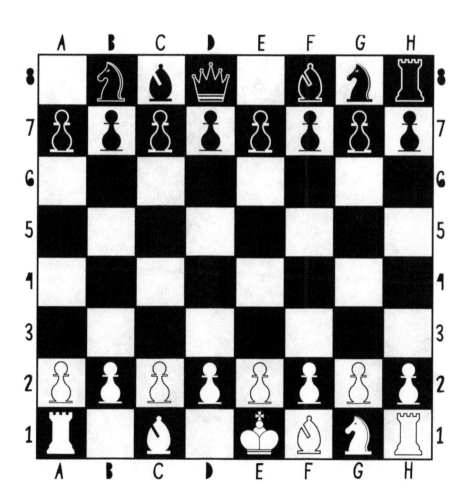

What path do you think the black Queen would follow to get to the shaded square?

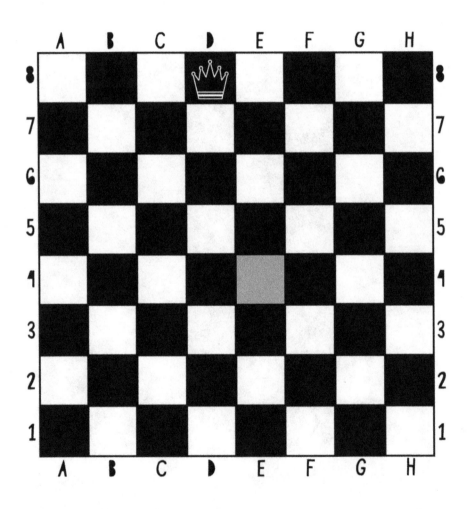

What path do you think the white Knight would follow to get to the shaded square?

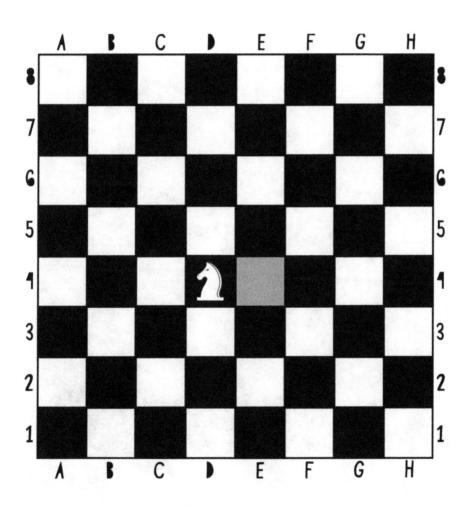

What path do you think the black Bishop would follow to get to the shaded square?

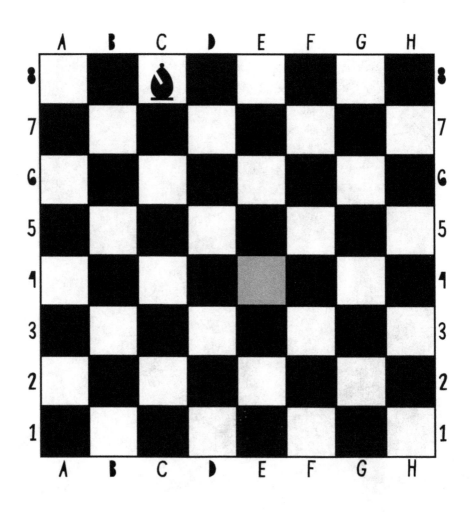

Wow! You are doing great. I hope you are having fun. Are you ready to learn more things? Follow me!

Chapter 2
Basic Concepts

In this chapter you are going to learn the value of each piece and some basic concepts, like capturing, check and checkmate. You will also learn how to play chess with points, just like in a tournament.

Let's go!

Value of the Pieces

In chess, each piece is assigned a relative value that tells you its strength. That value depends on the way they move and their offensive and defensive ability.

The value of the chess pieces is expressed in points. So allowing one of your pieces to be captured in order to capture another that's worth lesser points is known as sacrificing.

Let's see all the pieces' value in the next chart.

♛	9 points
♜	5 points
♝	3 points
♞	3 points
♟	1 point
♚	Undefined

The exact value of the King is undefined because it has very limited moves (basically it can't do much but stand around and look important!) and, above all, because it can't be captured or sacrificed during the game without losing it.

Did you know that in chess we
capture each other to win the game?
Let's see how it works!

Captures

Each piece can capture its opponent's pieces if they are placed in a square within reach, taking into account the way they move.

Capturing a piece means moving one of yours to the same square that piece is in - that way you take its place and eliminate that piece of your opponent from the game. One less piece for them to play with.

Now let's see how can a King, Queen, Bishop, Knight, Rook and Pawn capture their opponents.

Kings can capture and take the place of pieces placed one square away in any direction - remember, they can't move far.

Queens can capture pieces any number of squares away in any direction, they just can't jump over other pieces.

Bishops can capture pieces any number of squares away, but following only diagonal paths and without jumping.

Knights can capture pieces that fit into their L o 3x2 moving pattern, even jumping over other pieces.

Rooks can capture pieces any number of squares forward, backward, to their left or right, without jumping.

Pawns don't capture other pieces in the same way that they move around the board. They have a special way. Do you want to see how?

Pawns can only move one step forward at a time, but when they want to capture, they take one step diagonally to their left or right.

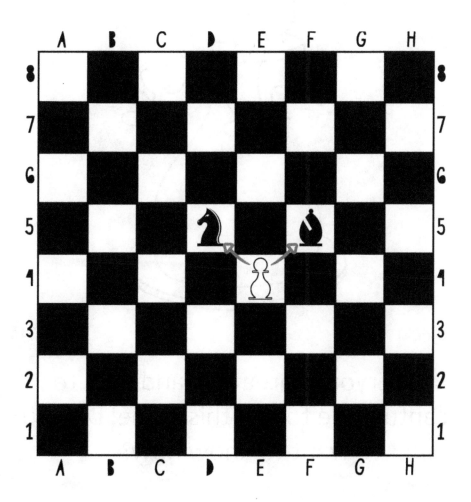

Everyone threatens and tries to capture me to win this game! Do you want to know how?

Check & Checkmate

A move that threatens the King is called a 'check' and it is mandatory to move the King that is being attacked. Think of it as moving the King away to a safe spot.

If there is no possible way to move the King to safety, it is called checkmate.

That's the goal of the game; the King in checkmate loses becausehe can find no space that is safe, and so their opponent wins the game.

Here are some examples of check and checkmate positions.

If the King moves to any other square, but F4, the Knight no longer threatens it, so this is just 'check' and the game can continue after moving the King to safety.

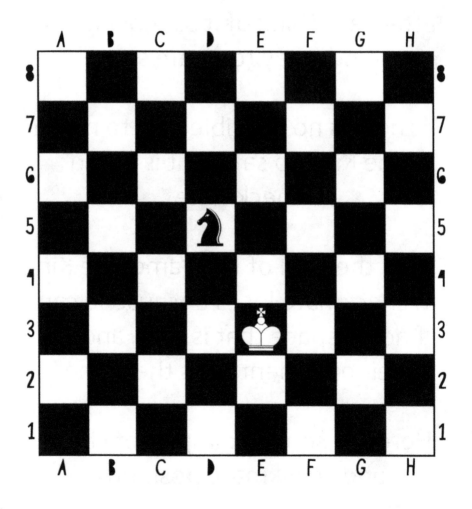

If the King moves to A2, the Rook is still attacking him, if it moves to B1, the Queen still threatens it, and if it moves to B2, the Bishop captures it. So this is 'checkmate.' The King has nowhere to go.

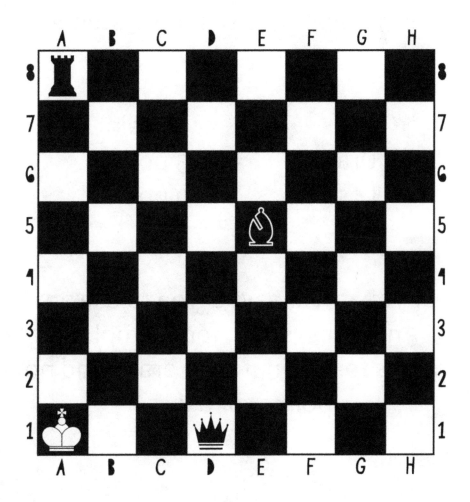

Scores

If you want to play chess with your family or friends as if you were in a tournament, you just need to remember this scoring system:

Win	1 point
Draw	0.5 points
Loss	0 points

Or you can always agree to use any Another system, for example, 3 points for a win, 1 for a draw, and no points for a loss.

There are several ways a game can end in a draw. One of them is called a stalemate, a situation where you are not in check, but can't make any move or else you would be in check. For example:

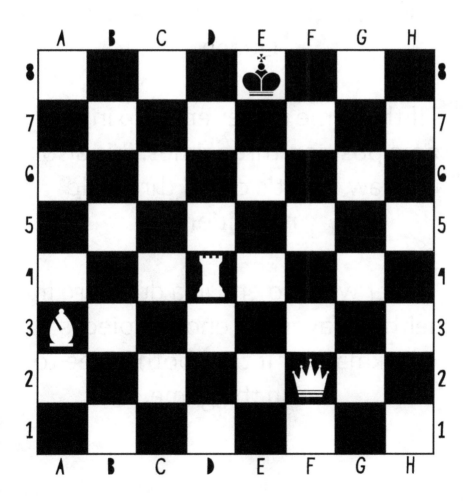

If the black King moves to D7 or D8, it is in check with the white Rook. If it moves to E7, it is in check with the white Bishop and if it moves to F7 or F8, it is in check with the white Queen.

If the same player ends up in the same position three times, it is also a draw and it's called threefold repetition.

Other ways to end in a draw are if neither player has enough pieces to checkmate or if they both agree to finish the game.

Exercises

Now that you've learned a lot of new concepts, how about a few activities to help you remember everything? Besides, I bet you are bursting to play!

Ready, steady... Go!

Choose the correct answer:

#1 When you are not in check, but can't move any piece, it is called...

☐ Checkmate
☐ Stalemate
☐ Capture

#2 When one of your opponent's pieces occupies the same square as one of your pieces, it is a...

☐ Capture
☐ Check
☐ Checkmate

Take a moment to remember how each piece moves and decide: is this check or checkmate?

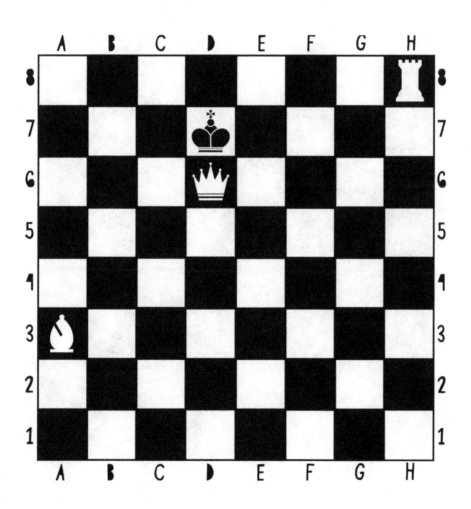

You need to keep the King safe without moving it, what piece can help you?

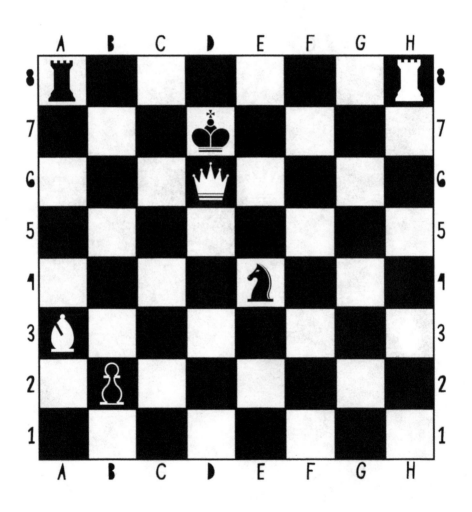

What Would You Do?

In this section there can be one or more than one correct answer and it's up to you to choose it. You can move the pieces as you like and in as many ways as you want.

Have fun!

White pieces move: Taking into account each piece's value, which one should the white Knight capture?

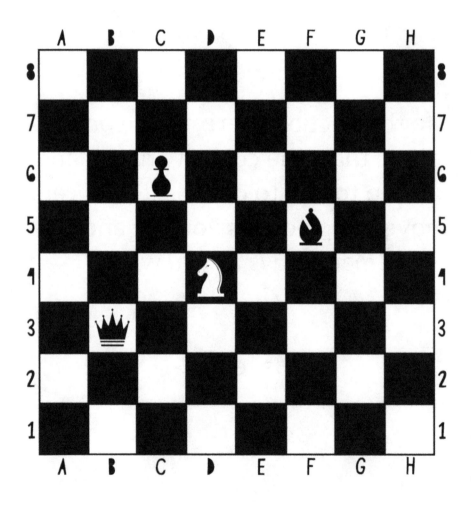

Black pieces move: The black King is under attack! Help him. Where would you put it to avoid that threat?

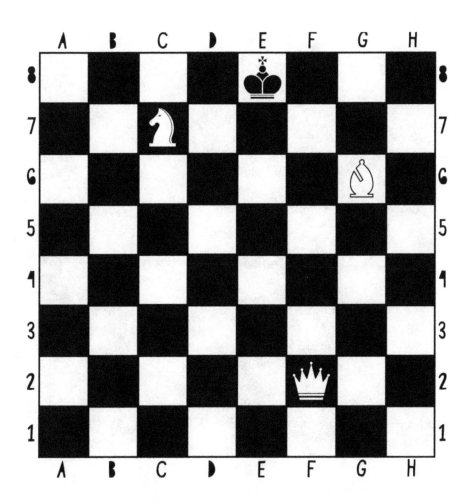

White pieces move: The white King is under attack, what would you do to protect it?

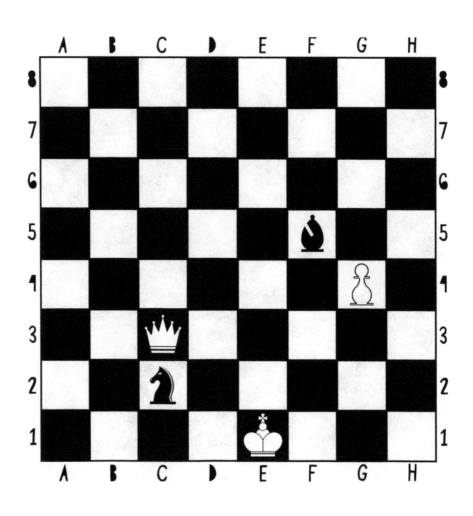

Wow! You are learning really fast. Remember to practice everything we havegone over. Do you want to learn some more? Let's go to the next chapter!

Chapter 3
Special Moves

There are three special moves in chess. In this chapter you are going to learn those moves and the pieces allowed to make them: Pawns, Kings and Rooks.

The three special moves are: 'en passant' and 'promotion' for Pawns and 'castling' for Kings and Rooks.

En passant

En passant is a move only Pawns can make. An en passant capture is when a Pawn captures another Pawn that takes two steps on its first move as it passes by.

En passant is French for 'in passing'.

It requires a Pawn that takes two initial steps and lands right next to an opposing Pawn (from now on, the capturing Pawn). At that point, the capturing Pawn can take a diagonal step and capture the other Pawn 'as it passes by'.

There are some conditions to make an en passant capture:

#1 The capturing Pawn must be in its 5th rank, that is rank number 5 for white Pawns and number 4 for black Pawns.

#2 The captured Pawn must take two steps on its initial move.

#3 The en passant capture has to be made immediately after the two-step move, otherwise you lose that opportunity.

Let's see this move from the white pieces' point of view. If the white Pawn takes two steps and lands right next to the black Pawn, from B2 to B4, then the black Pawn is allowed to take a diagonal step from A4 to B3 and capture the white Pawn as it passes by on its way to B4.

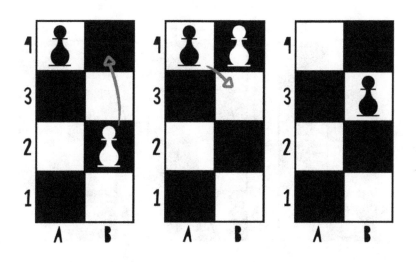

And now let's see this move from the black pieces' point of view. If the black Pawn takes two steps and lands right next to the white Pawn, from B7 to B5, then the white Pawn is allowed to take a diagonal step from A5 to B6 and capture the black Pawn as it passes by on its way to B5.

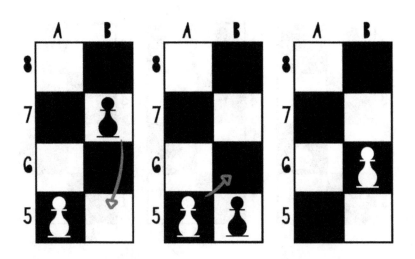

I look good with the Queen's crown, right?

I can also make a great Rook, Bishop or Knight!

Promotion

Remember how the Pawn has the special ability to turn into another piece? Well if a Pawn manages to reach the other side of the board, that is, if a white Pawn reaches rank number 8 and a black one reaches rank number 1, they earn the right to become any piece of their choice, except a King.

That ability to become a piece of higher value, be it a Knight, Bishop, Rook, or Queen, is known as 'promotion'. There's no limit in terms of pieces, so the same player can have, for example, two or more Queens! Now that could get interesting!

Generally, Pawns are promoted to Queens (also called 'queening') because they are the most valuable pieces. Why are they the most valuable? Because they can do whatever they like, apart from jumping. Choosing any other piece is also known as 'underpromotion.'

Knight underpromotions are the most common because they have the most distinctive moves.

When a Pawn can be promoted but will be captured immediately after being promoted, it is not necessary to choose a powerful piece, which is known as 'insignificant underpromotion.'

Did you know that you can build a fortress around the King to protect it? Fortresses are often built around Kings to protect them, and now you can build one in chess.

Castling

'Castling' is the most common special chess move and involves the King and one of its Rooks.

Castling is the only move that allows two pieces to move during the same turn and is also the only situation where a Rook can jump. You can imagine the Rook gets a bit excited to have a chance to jump!

There are two types of castling, depending on the Rook that is going to protect the King and the number of steps it needs to take: short or kingside and long or queenside.

Castling kingside means that the Rook involved is the one closest to the King, that is, the Rook on the H-file.

It is also called short castling because the Rook only needs to take two steps to protect the King.

Castling queenside means that the Rook involved is the one closest to the Queen, that is, the Rook on the A-file.

It is also called long castling because the Rook needs to take three steps to protect the King.

Castling is only allowed if:

#1 The King and Rook have not moved during the game. It is not allowed if they have already moved, even if they have returned to their initial position.

#2 There isn't any piece between the King and Rook, because the King can't jump and the Rook can only jump over the King while castling.

#3 The King is not in check, any of the squares that it needs to move through are under attack and will not end up in check either.

When castling kingside: the white King takes two steps from E1 to G1 and the white Rook also takes two steps, jumping over the King, from H1 to F1.

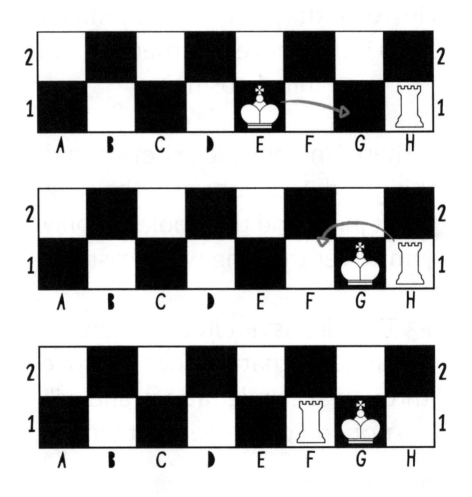

And, also castling kingside, the black King takes two steps from E8 to G8 and the black Rook takes two steps, jumping over the King, from H8 to F8.

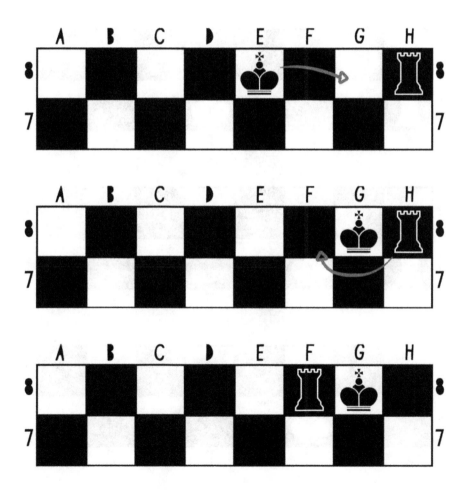

When castling queenside: the white King takes two steps from E1 to C1 and the white Rook takes three steps, jumping over the King, from A1 to D1.

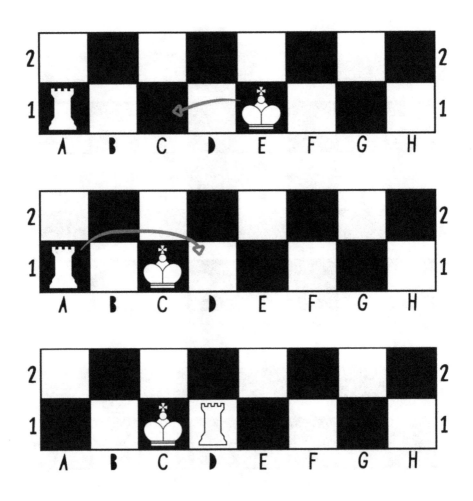

And, also castling queenside: the black King takes two steps from E8 to C8 and the black Rook takes three steps, jumping over the King, from A8 to D8.

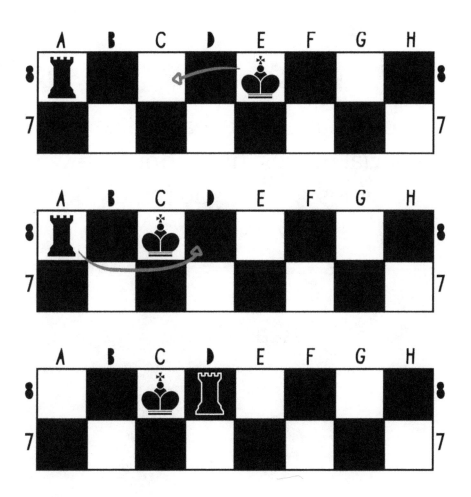

Exercises

Now that you've learned some special moves, how about a few activities to help you remember everything?

Ready? Go!

Choose the correct answer:

#1 When a Rook jumps over the King to protect it, it is called...

- ☐ Promotion
- ☐ En passant capture
- ☐ Castling

#2 When you capture one of your opponent's Pawns as it passes by one of your own Pawns, it is called...

- ☐ Promotion
- ☐ En passant capture
- ☐ Castling

#3 When a Pawn moves far enough to reach the other side of the board, it gets promoted and can become a...

- ☐ Queen
- ☐ Rook
- ☐ Bishop
- ☐ Knight
- ☐ All of them

#4 Castling is a special move that can be made...

- ☐ Kingside
- ☐ Queenside
- ☐ Both

Look at these three steps, from top to bottom, and circle the special move you see:

En passant   Castling   Promotion

Look at these three steps, from left to right, and circle the special move you see:

En passant   Castling   Promotion

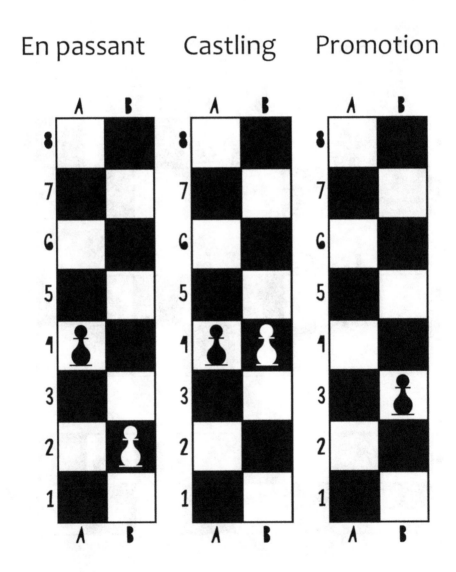

Look at these three steps, from top to bottom, and circle the special move you see:

En passant   Castling   Promotion

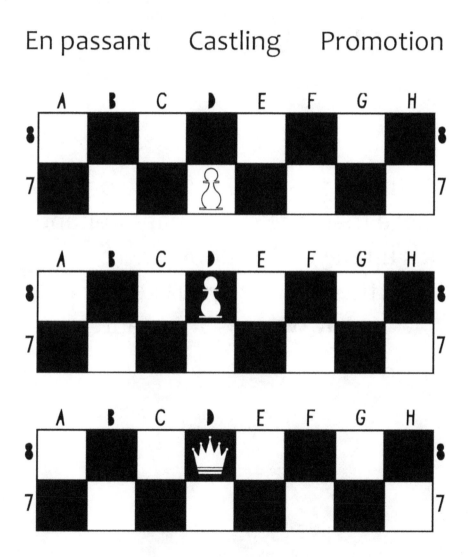

What Would You Do?

In this section there can be one or more than one correct answer and it's up to you to choose it. You can move the pieces as you like and in as many ways as you want.

Have fun!

What piece would you promote your white Pawn to or which one would you move to put the black King in check?

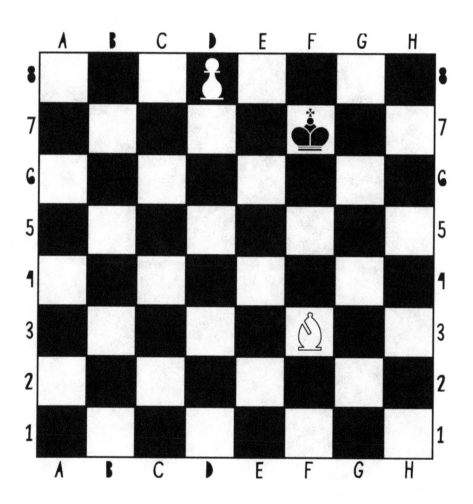

The white Pawn on D4 just took two steps. Taking into account each piece's value, where would you place the black Pawn on C4?

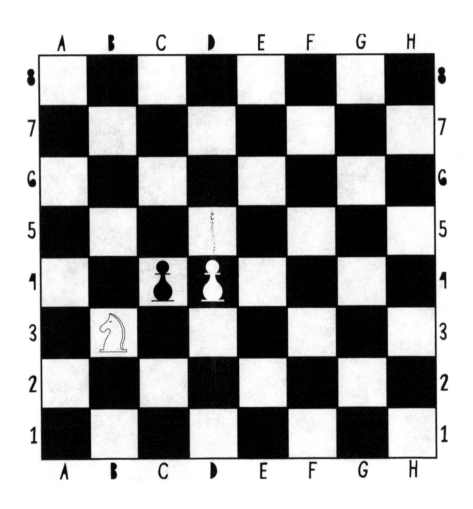

Do you like my Bishop hat? I think I'll keep it on while you learn some tactics... They are quite useful!

Chapter 4
Basic Tactics

In this chapter, you are going to learn three basic tactics to force your opponent to move certain pieces or limit their moves to capture them. In other words, I'm going to teach you how to be tricksy!

These tactics are known as pins, forks, and skewers, depending on the number and value of the pieces under attack.

Pins

When you attack a lesser value piece and your opponent has to sacrifice it because moving it would mean exposing a higher value piece, it is called a 'pin.'

The piece under attack is being pinned and the attacking one is known as the pinning piece.

The only pieces allowed to make a pin are those who can move any number of steps in any direction.

There are three types of pins: absolute, relative, and partial.

If the pinned piece is protecting the King from the pinning one, it is an absolute pin, as it is illegal to move the pinned piece and put the King in check.

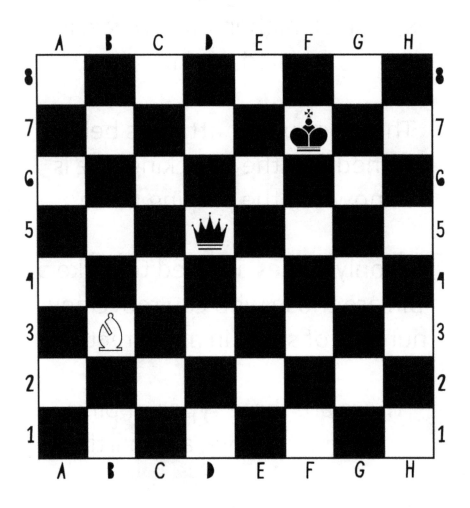

If the pinned piece is shielding any other piece, but still a more valuable piece than the pinned one, it is a relative pin. You can either move or sacrifice it.

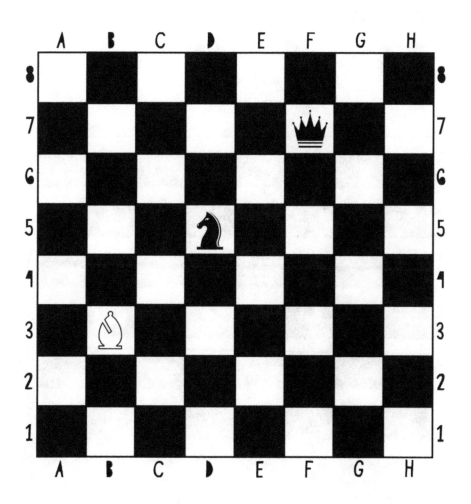

If a Queen, Rook, or Bishop are pinned along a rank, file, or diagonal, it is a partial pin because they are still able to move along those paths. In this case, the white Rook can move along the 3rd rank without exposing the Queen.

Snack time! Did you know that forks and skewers are also used in chess? Chess is full of surprises and that is why I love it!

Forks

When you attack two or more of your opponent's pieces at the same time with the same piece, it is called a 'fork.' The piece under attack is being forked and the attacking one is known as the forking piece.

Any piece can fork, however, the most important forking piece is the Knight.

There are many types of forks, depending on the pieces under attack. Some examples are the royal fork, grand fork, or family fork.

If your forking piece, for example, a Knight, is attacking your opponent's King and Queen at the same time, it is called a royal fork.

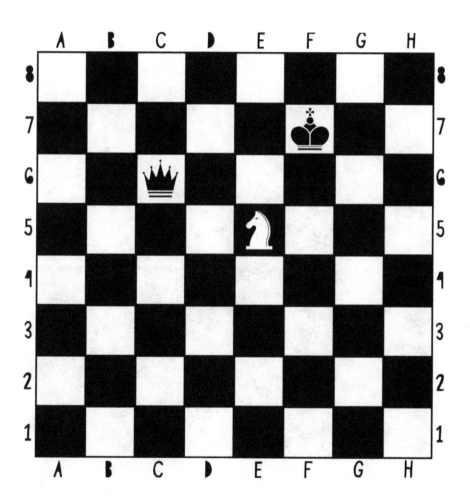

If your forking piece, for example, a Knight, is attacking your opponent's King, Queen, and one or both Rooks at the same time, it is called a grand fork.

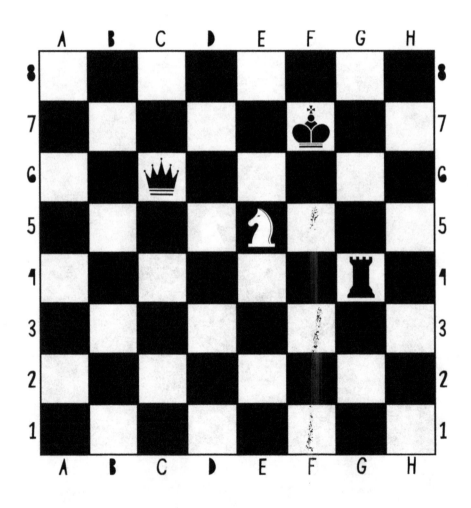

If your forking piece, for example, a Knight, is attacking your opponent's King, Queen, and any other piece at the same time, it is called a family fork.

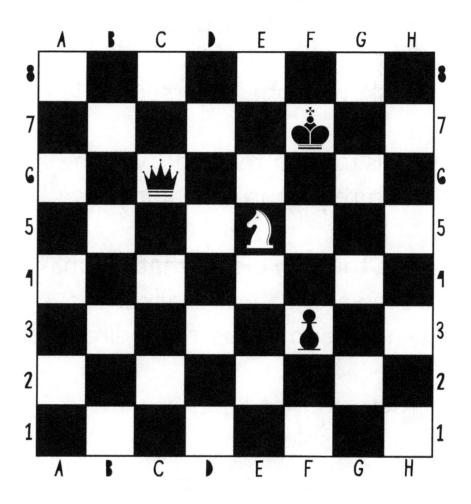

Skewers

When you attack a higher value piece and your opponent has to sacrifice or move it, exposing a lesser value piece, it is called a 'skewer' or a 'reversed pin.'

This tactic often ends with the capture of more valuable pieces.

Again, the only pieces that can make a skewer are those that can move any number of steps in any direction.

There are two types of skewers: absolute and relative.

If the King is under attack, it is an 'absolute skewer' because it is mandatory to move the King to safety, exposing the piece it was shielding.

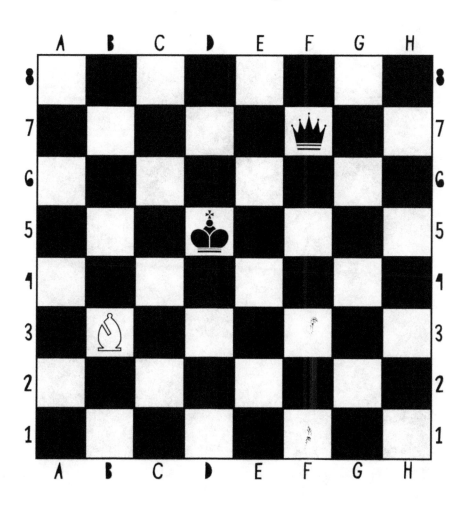

If there is any other piece being skewered, it is a relative skewer. You can either move the piece or sacrifice it to protect the one it was shielding.

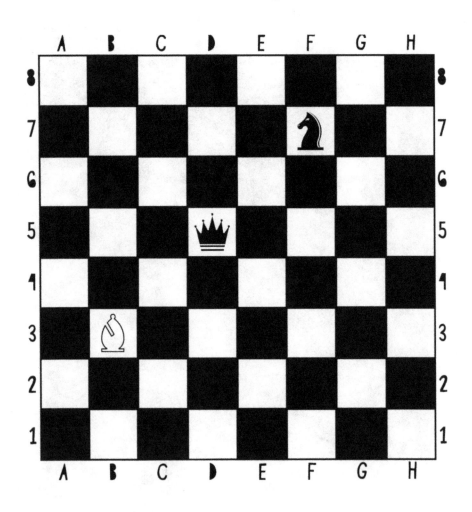

Exercises

Now that you've learned some basic tactics, how about a few activities to help you remember them?

Ready, steady... Go!

Choose the correct answer:

#1 If you attack a Queen that is shielding a Bishop, it is called...

- ☐ Relative skewer
- ☐ Relative pin
- ☐ Absolute skewer

#2 If you attack a Bishop that is shielding a King, it is called...

- ☐ Absolute pin
- ☐ Absolute skewer
- ☐ Relative pin

#3 If you prevent a Queen from advancing to another rank, but it can still move along that rank, it is called...

- ☐ Relative pin
- ☐ Partial pin
- ☐ Absolute pin

#4 If you attack a King and Queen at the same time with the same piece, it is called...

- ☐ Family fork
- ☐ Royal fork
- ☐ Grand fork

Can you find all 9 words related to the tactics in this word search puzzle?

```
P  I  N  Y  F  O  R  K  T  G
A  B  O  M  J  G  T  S  D  R
R  R  E  L  A  T  I  V  E  A
T  K  E  U  R  O  Y  A  L  N
I  X  T  Z  E  A  N  P  A  D
A  B  S  O  L  U  T  E  W  P
L  I  F  A  M  I  L  Y  N  B
S  K  E  W  E  R  T  G  E  K
```

Now, choose a piece to fork the black King, Queen and Bishop at the same time:

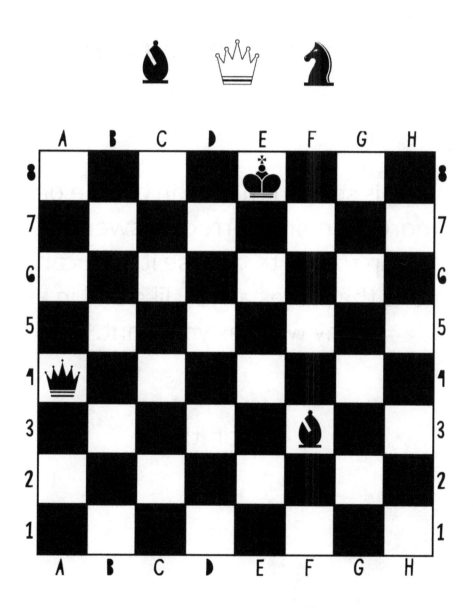

What Would You Do?

In this section there can be one or more than one correct answer and it's up to you to choose it. You can move the pieces as you like and in as many ways as you want.

Go for it!

Black pieces move: What would you do to pin the white Knight and King?

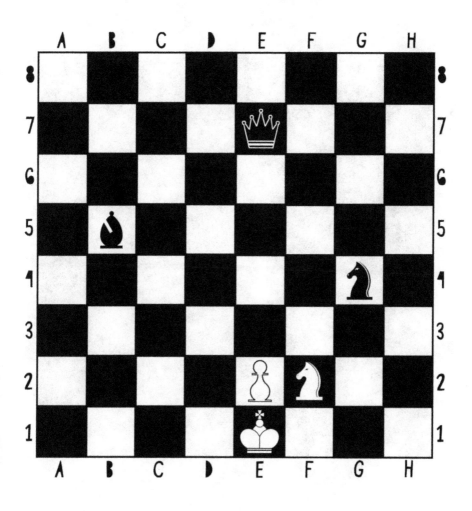

Black pieces move: What would you do to fork the white Pawn and Bishop?

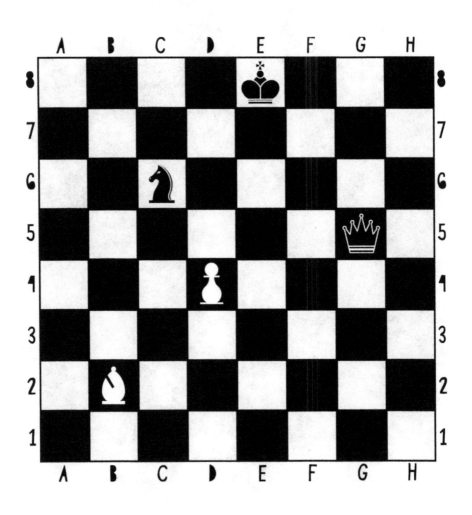

Black pieces move: What would you do to turn this skewer into a pin?

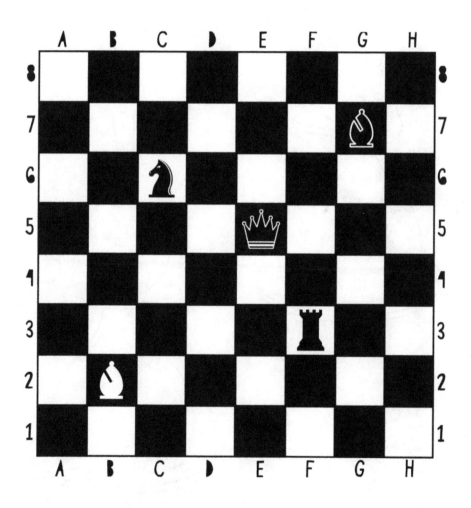

What should we
learn next?

Oh, I know!
Openings!

Chapter 5
Opening Moves

In chess, the white pieces always start the game. The first move a player makes is known as 'opening'. In this chapter, you are going to learn the best and most common openings.

White and also black pieces have 20 moves to choose from at the beginning of the game, 16 with Pawns and 4 with Knights.

The most common openings involve: the white Pawns on D2, the Queen's Pawn, and E2, the King's Pawn.

On the other side of the board, the most common moves in response involve: the black Pawns on D7 and E7.

Each first step leads to a series of opening moves that have been developed throughout the years.

Learning those techniques can help you start the game on the right foot and win.

White King's Pawn

Starting the game by taking two steps with the white King's Pawn, from E2 to E4, is the first step in a series of opening moves. Some of these moves are: the 'Ruy Lopez', the 'Italian Game' and the 'Sicilian Defense.'

These are the most common openings, but there are many more that you can learn as you grow as a chess player.

Also, all these openings have multiple variations, always depending on the player's strategy plan.

Ruy Lopez

This opening move, also known as the 'Spanish Game', is named after the 16th-century Spanish priest who studied it. Interesting, huh?

This initial move does not pose an immediate threat to the black pieces, and that is why there are many and very different possible responses.

The advantages of this technique are well balanced: the white pieces weaken the black Pawns' structure and the black pieces gain attack space.

In the 'Ruy Lopez' opening, the first move is taking the white King's Pawn from E2 to E4, followed by the black King's Pawn from E7 to E5.

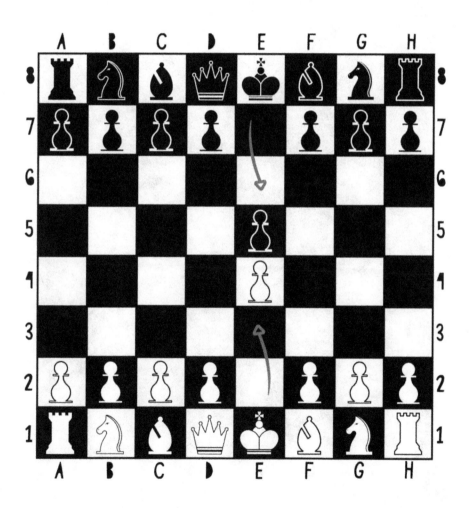

The next steps are moving the white Knight on G1 to F3 and then the black Knight on B8 to C6, each of them jumping over a Pawn.

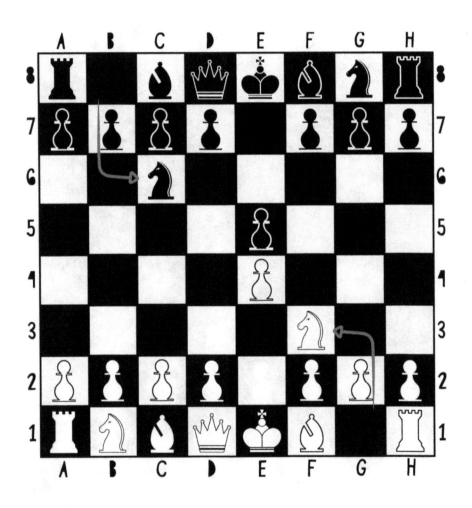

The last step of this opening is moving the white Bishop on F1 to B5. Moving the white Pawn on the first step clears the way for the Bishop.

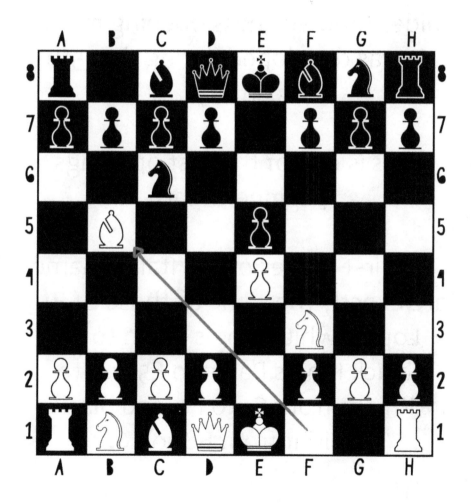

Italian Game

The 'Italian opening', 'Italian Game' or 'Italian Defense' is probably the oldest known chess opening move. It was developed during the 15th century.

This is one of the first openings beginners learn.

The first moves of the Italian Game are exactly the same as those of Ruy Lopez: white King's Pawn to E4, black King's Pawn to E5, white Knight from G1 to F3, and black Knight from B8 to C6.

The difference between the Italian Game and the Ruy Lopez opening is their third move. In this case, the white Bishop on F1 is placed on C4.

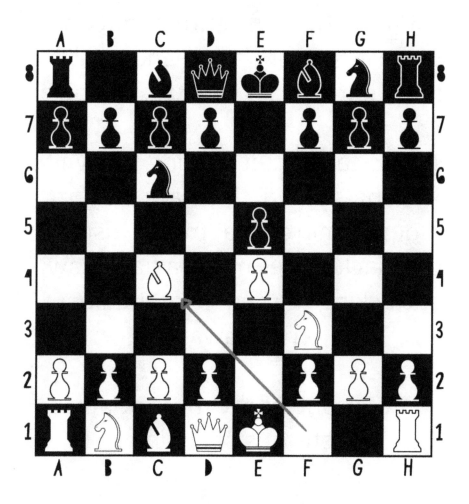

Sicilian Defense

The 'Sicilian Defense' dates back to the late 16th century, although it was not until the 18th century that it was given its current name and until the 20th century that it became popular.

In this case, after moving the white King's Pawn, the black player doesn't mirror that move. Instead, the black pieces move a flank Pawn, attacking the center of the board right away.

This is one of the most popular defenses of all time.

After moving the white King's Pawn from E2 to E4, the black Pawn on C7 moves to C5. It is a very flexible defense that allows many variations.

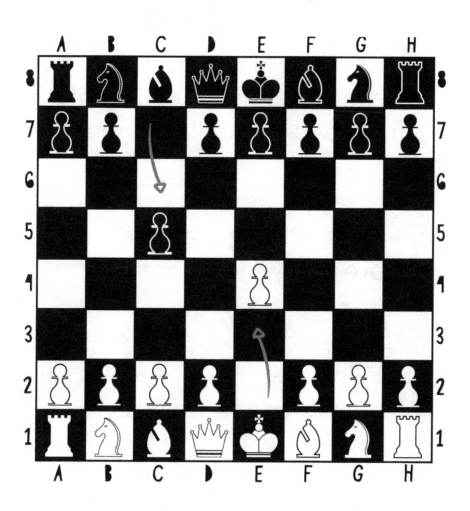

White Queen's Pawn

Starting the game by taking two steps with the white Queen's Pawn, from D2 to D4, is also the first step in a series of opening moves. Some of these moves are: the 'Queen's Gambit' and the 'Indian Defenses.'

These are the most common openings, but there are also many more that you can learn later.

Again, all these openings have multiple variations, depending on the player's strategy plan.

Queen's Gambit

When a player makes an opening that involves sacrificing a piece, usually a Pawn, it is known as a 'gambit.'

The 'Queen's Gambit' is one of the oldest and most used openings, that is why there are so many variations.

It is called a gambit because a white Pawn is offered for capture. The black player can choose to capture it (Queen's Gambit accepted) or ignore it (Queen's Gambit declined).

The first step in the Queen's Gambit is moving the white Queen's Pawn from D2 to D4 and the black Queen's Pawn from D7 to D5.

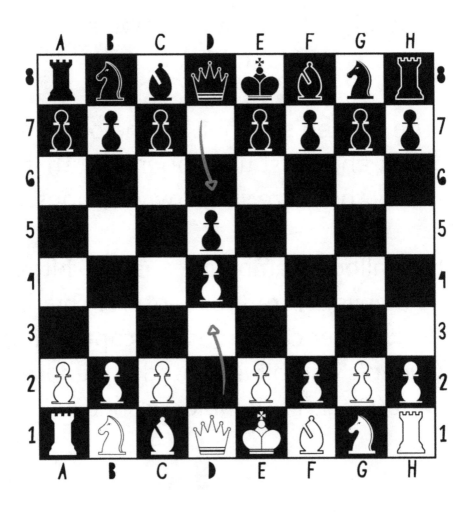

The next step is moving the white Pawn on C2 to C4. Now, the black player can choose between capturing it or developing another strategy.

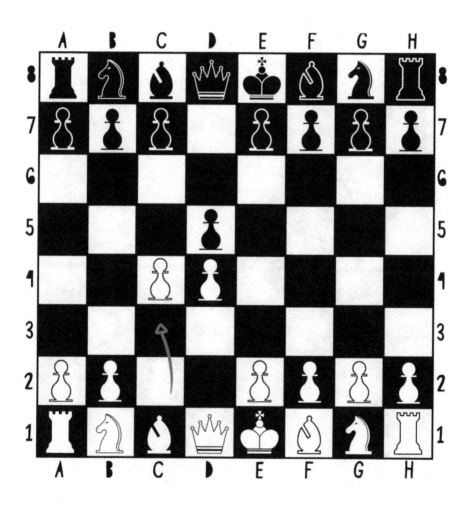

If the black Pawn captures it, the gambit is accepted. Now, the white Pawn on E2 can move to E3, so the Bishop on F1 attacks the black Pawn.

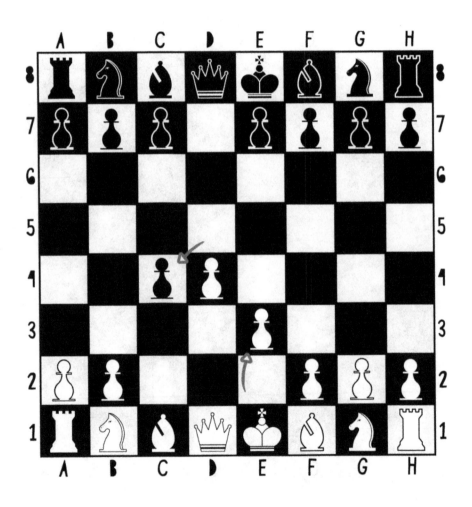

If the black Pawn doesn't capture it, the gambit is declined. In this situation, moving the black Pawn on E7 to E6 reinforces the Pawn structure.

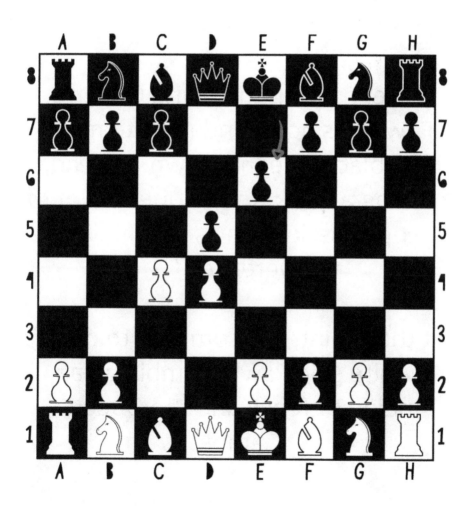

Indian Defenses

The concept of 'Indian Defense' was born in the late 19th century and the name comes from the openings used by an Indian player.

After moving the white Queen's Pawn, it's not mandatory to move the black Queen's Pawn. Instead, moving a black Knight opens a lot of options, known as the 'Indian Defenses.'

At that point, it is common to offer a white side Pawn, combining an Indian Defense and the Queen's Gambit.

After the white Queen's Pawn moves from D2 to D4, the black Knight on G8 jumps to F6. The next move leads to many different defenses.

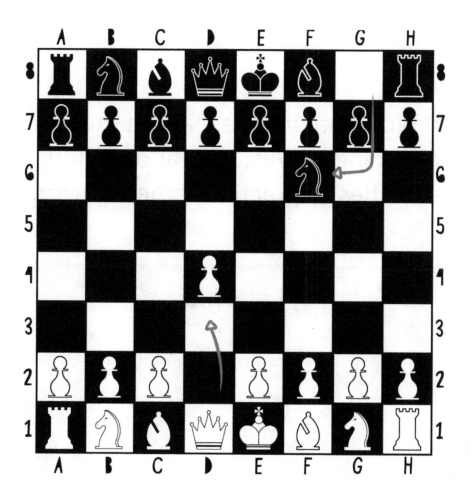

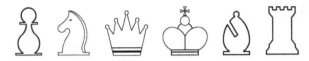

Exercises

Now that you've learned these opening moves, how about a few activities to practice some of them?

Let's go!

Match each opening technique with
the first piece that moves:

Queen's
Gambit

Italian
Game

Sicilian
Defense

Queen's Pawn to D4	King's Pawn to E4

Ruy
Lopez

Indian
Defenses

In which opening techniques do the black pieces mirror the first move of the white pieces? That is, they move the black Queen's Pawn after the white one and the black King's Pawn after the white one.

☐ Ruy Lopez
☐ Italian Game
☐ Sicilian Defense
☐ Queen's Gambit
☐ Indian Defenses

What Would You Do?

In this section, there can be one or more than one correct answer and it's up to who to choose it? You! Move the pieces as you like and in as many ways as you want.

Go!

Black pieces move: What piece would you move to make this opening an Indian Defense?

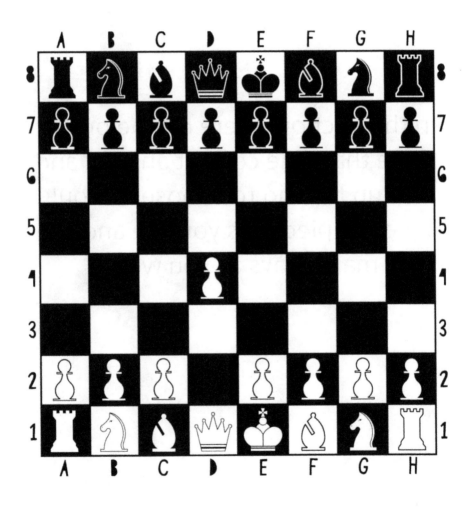

White pieces move: What piece would you move to make this opening a Queen's Gambit?

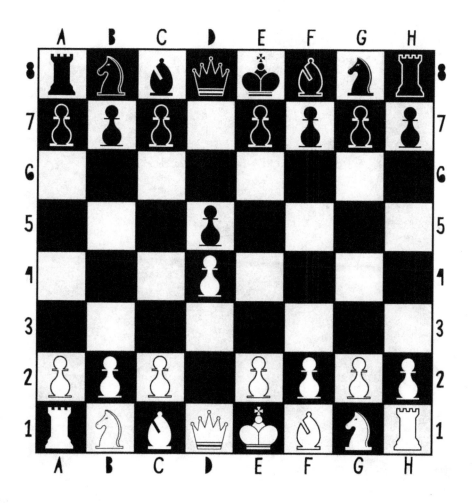

White pieces move: Where would you place the Bishop on F1 to make this opening a Ruy Lopez?

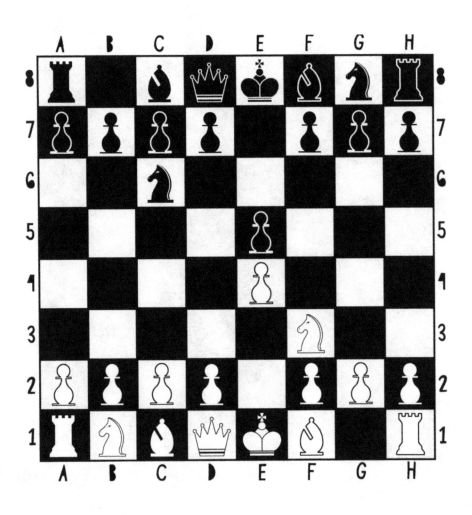

White pieces move: Where would
you place the Bishop on F1 to make
this opening an Italian Game?

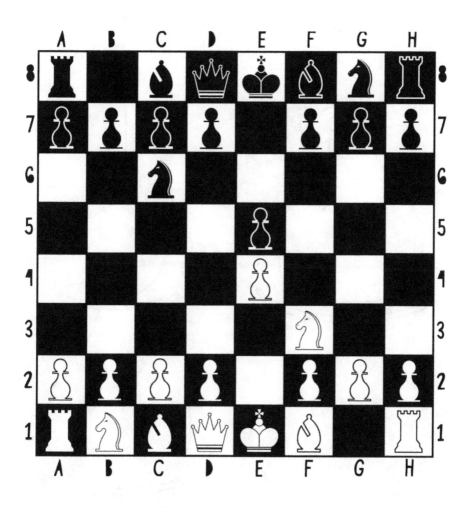

Chapter 6
Checkmates

In this chapter, you are going to learn five important checkmate techniques. These techniques involve just two pieces, besides the King in checkmate.

Depending on the technique, the pieces involved are Queen and Rook, Queen and Knight, Queen and Bishop, Bishop and Knight, and King and Pawn.

With just your Queen and a Rook you can win this game!

Queen and Rook

A Queen and a Rook can easily work together to checkmate a King.

If a King hasn't moved from the edge of the board or has moved and returned, it's easy to corner it with one of these two pieces and checkmate it with the other.

The Rook can prevent the King from advancing to the next rank, blocking its escape, while the Queen can also move towards the edge of the board and checkmate it.

The black Rook on B2 prevents the white King from advancing to any of the squares on the second rank, keeping it trapped on the edge of the board.

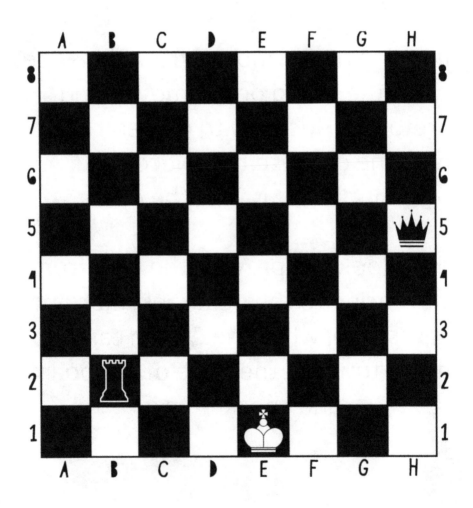

If the black Queen moves to the first rank, regardless of the square, as long as it is safe from the white King, the King has nowhere to go. Checkmate!

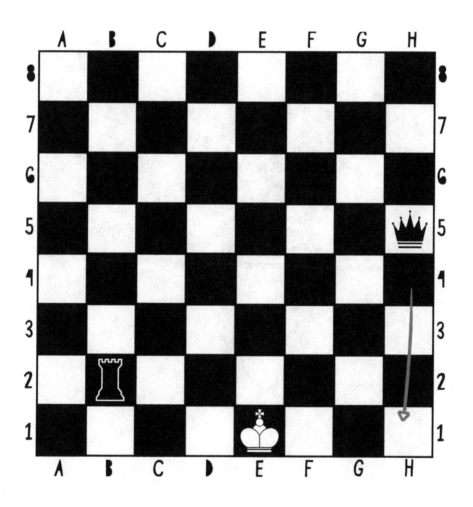

It can also be done the other way around: the Queen stays on the second rank, keeping the King trapped, while the Rook advances to the first rank.

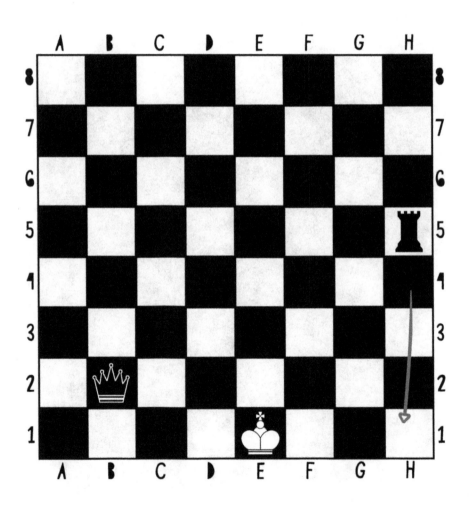

You can also use your Queen and a
Knight!

Queen and Knight

Just like in the case of the Queen and Rook working together, the key is trapping the King on the edge of the board. Although the Queen and Knight are the ones directly involved in this checkmate, they might need a Rook's help to do that.

In this case, the Queen moves right in front of the King. The Knight should be placed one move away from the Queen, that way the King can't escape or capture the Queen either.

If the white King is on the edge of the board, moving the black Queen to E2 puts it in checkmate, because the King can't move to D1, D2, F1, or F2.

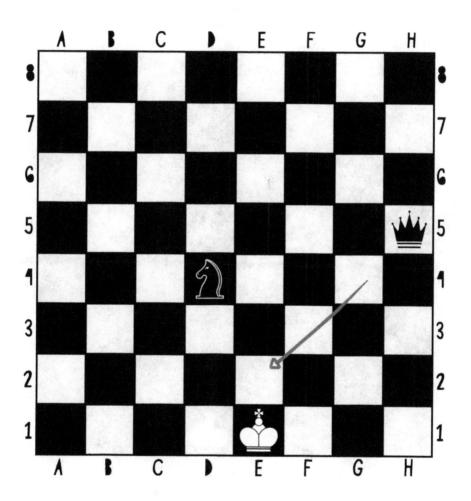

The white King could capture the black Queen, but the black Knight on D4 is protecting it and that would put the King in check, which is not allowed.

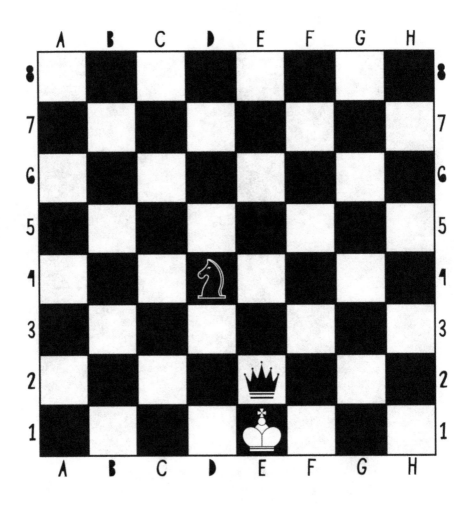

The Queen and a Bishop are also
good allies to win the game!

Queen and Bishop

The Queen and Bishop can work together exactly like the previous case, except that they don't need a Rook. The Queen 'checkmates' the King while the Bishop protects it.

In order to win the game, the Queen moves right in front of the King, while the Bishop stays away protecting it, so the King under attack can't capture the Queen.

This technique works whether the King is being shielded or not.

Moving the white Queen to E7 puts the black King in checkmate because the white Bishop on B4 protects it from being captured by the King.

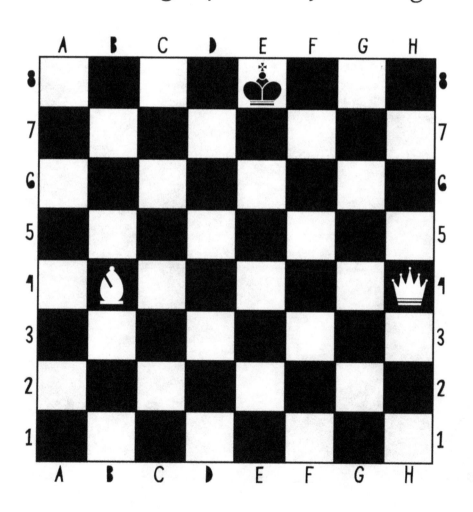

If the black King is, for example, castled and surrounded by Pawns, this strategy works too. Moving the white Queen to G7 does the trick.

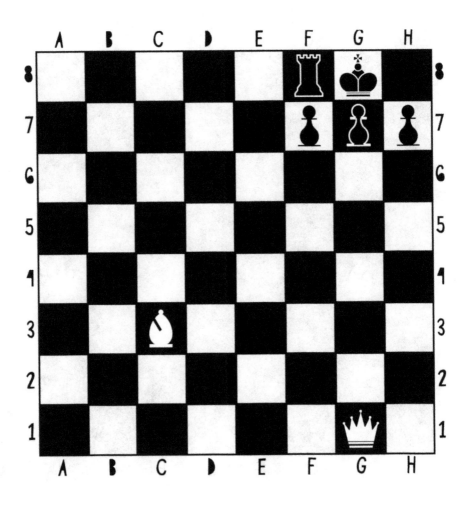

How about we let the Queen rest?
Let's work with a Bishop and a
Knight!

Bishop and Knight

This type of checkmate relies on the help, sometimes involuntary, of other pieces, whether they are of the same color or those of the opposite color.

A Bishop and a Knight can force a checkmate together, but usually not on their own. They often take advantage of the position of the pieces that are defending their opponent's King, because shielding it can also block most of the King's escape routes. They can also lean on other pieces of their own set.

If the black King is surrounded by black Pawns that have not yet moved and castled, the white Bishop can prevent it from moving to squares G7 or H8.

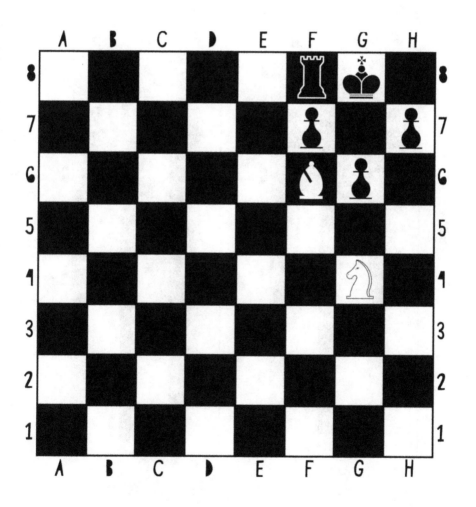

Moving the black Knight from G4 to H6 puts the white King in checkmate because it can't move and the Knight can jump over the black Pawn in H7.

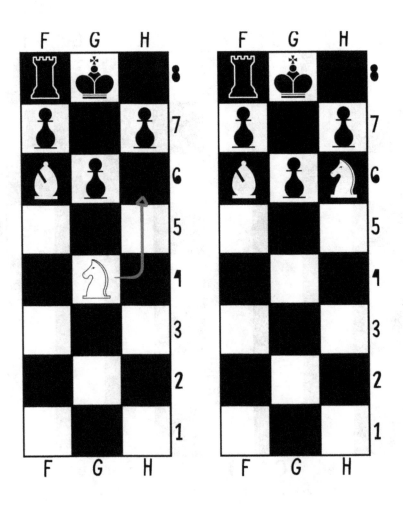

Kings and Pawns work well together too!

King and Pawn

This technique proves that even the least valuable piece, a Pawn, can be quite useful, *and* surprising. A Pawn can be as good an attacker as any other piece and, combined with the King, can easily checkmate your opponent.

If, for example, the white King is trying to avoid a black Pawn getting promoted and the black King is placed right behind it to support the Pawn, the white King is going to find itself trapped. If you attack the white King with another black Pawn, checkmate! Bye, bye King!

Here, the black Pawn on E2 prevents the white King from moving to D1 or F1 and the black King also prevents it from moving towards D2 and F2.

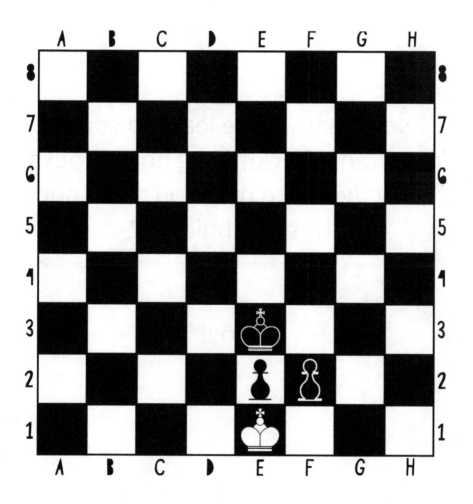

Exercises

Now that you've learned some
important checkmates, how about a
few activities to help you remember
those techniques?

Enjoy!

Can you tell, without looking back, which checkmates you just learned?

☐ King & Queen
☐ Queen & Bishop
☐ Rook & Pawn
☐ Pawn & King
☐ Queen & Rook
☐ Knight & King
☐ Bishop & Knight
☐ King & Rook
☐ Queen & Knight

What piece needs to go on F5 to checkmate the black King?

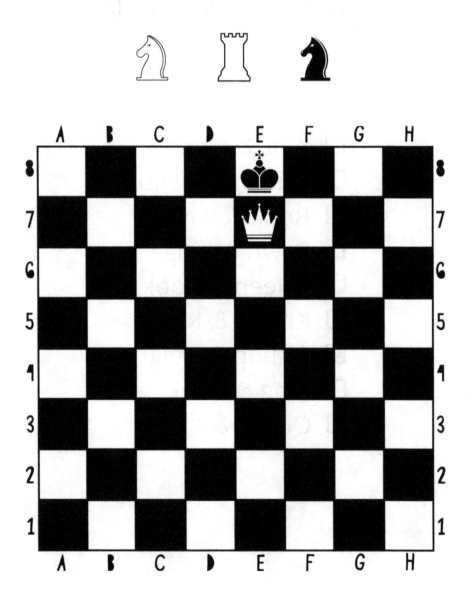

What piece needs to go on H1 to checkmate the white King?

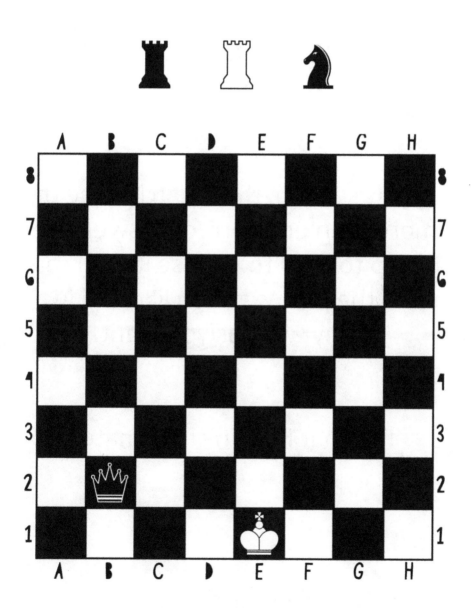

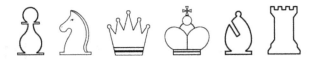

What Would You Do?

In this section, there can be one or more than one correct answer and it's up to YOU to choose it. You can move the pieces as you like and in as many ways as you want.

Put that King in checkmate!

White pieces move: What would you do to checkmate the black King?

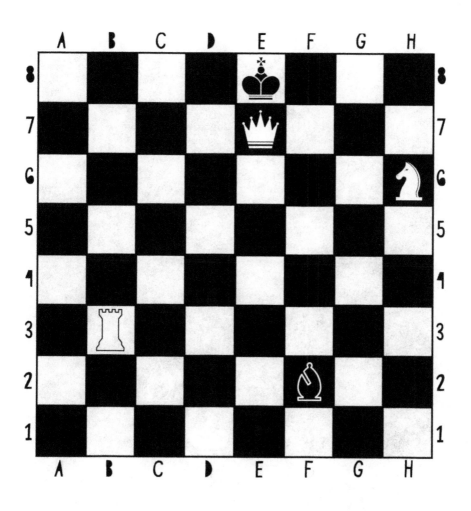

Black pieces move: What would you do to checkmate the white King?

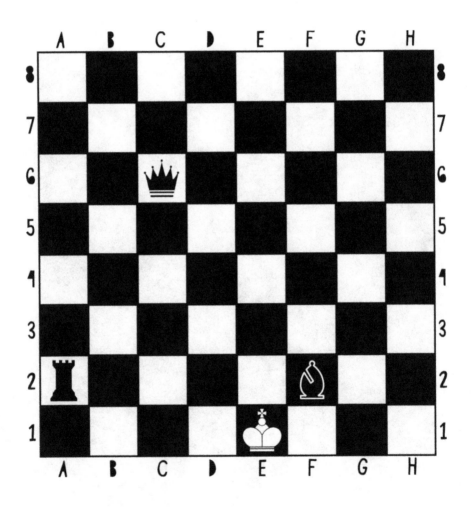

White pieces move: What would you do to checkmate the black King?

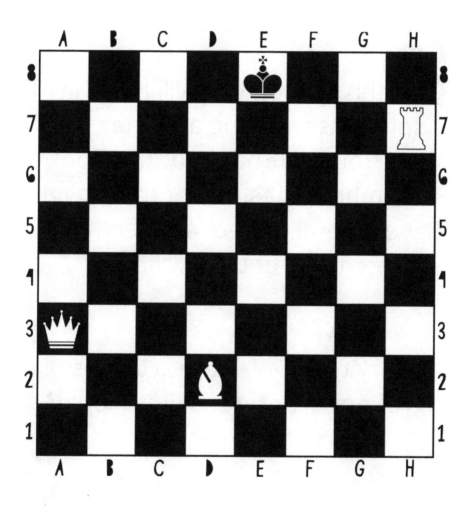

Solutions

In this section you will find the solutions to all the activities you have found throughuot this book. Remember that some of them might have several correct answers, all of them equally valid.

But try to solve all the activities on your own before taking a look!

Chapter 1: Board & Pieces

Match each piece on the left
with its name:

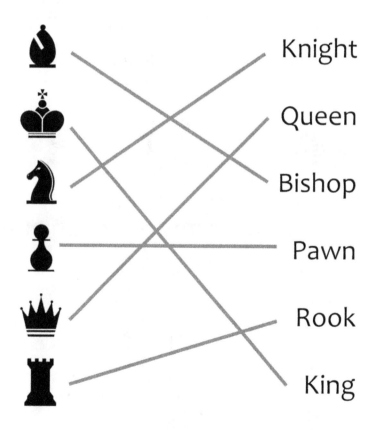

Who would say that? Read each sentence carefully and circle the piece who said it:

#1 I can take two steps forward on my first move.

#2 I can move in any direction and as many steps as I want.

#3 I can always jump over other pieces.

#4 I can move in any direction, but taking one step at a time.

#5 I can move back and forth, but just along diagonal paths.

Can you find all the pieces in this Word search puzzle? Remember, there are six different pieces.

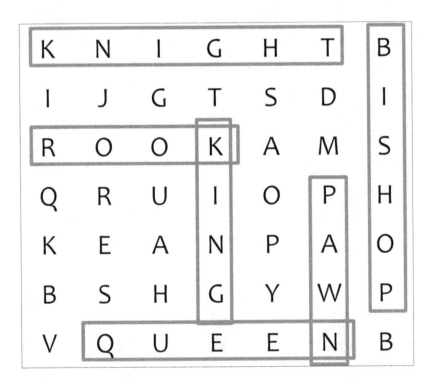

This board looks a little bit empty, how sad! Let's fill it up. Where would you place the missing Rook, Knight, King, and Queen?

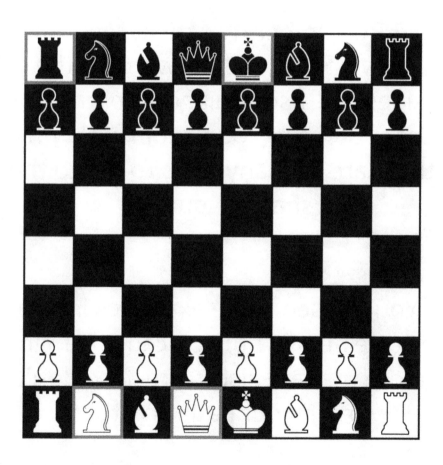

What path do you think the black Queen would follow to get to the shaded square?

→ Remember that the Queen can move backward, forward, to the sides and also in diagonal paths, as many steps as you need. That's why there are so many ways to get to the shaded square.

You can see some examples in the picture below, but you can find many more that are also correct, so don't worry if your path isn't there.

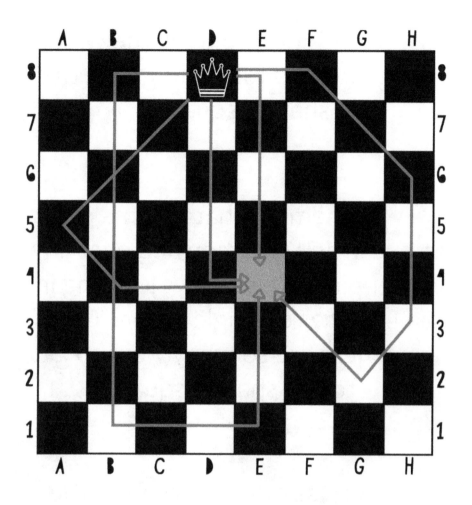

You can try as many times as you
want, discovering a new path each
time. Have fun!

What path do you think the white Knight would follow to get to the shaded square?

→ Remember that Knights can move in any direction and over any other piece, but always jumping in an L or 3x2 rectangle shape. That's why there are so many ways to get to the shaded square.

You can see one example in the picture below, but remember you can find many more that are also correct, so again don't worry if that's not the path you chose.

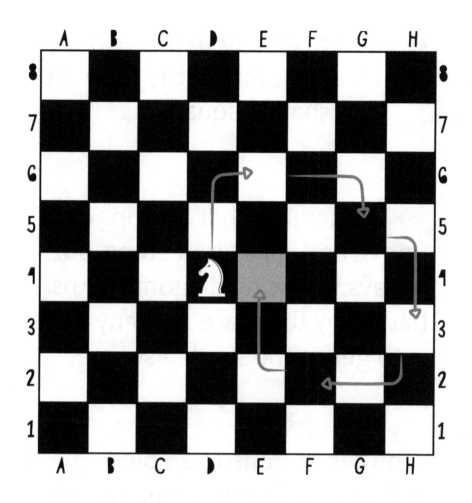

You can try as many times as you want, discovering a new path each time. How many can you find?

What path do you think the black Bishop would follow to get to the shaded square?

→ Remember that Bishops can move any number of steps, but always following diagonal paths. That's why there are so many ways to get to the shaded square.

You can see one example in the picture below, but remember you can find many more that are also correct, so again don't worry if that's not the path you chose.

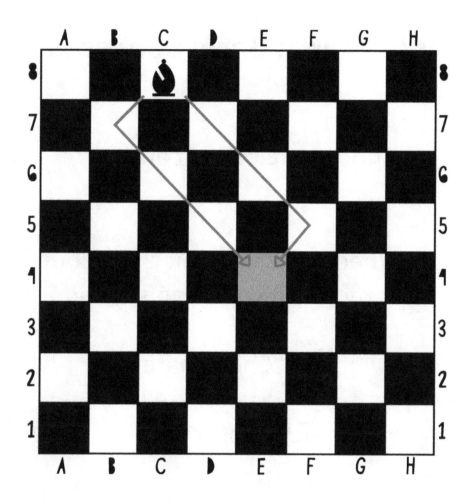

You can try as many times as you want, discovering a new path each time. Enjoy!

Chapter 2: Basic Concepts

Choose the correct answer:

#1 When you are not in check, but can't move any piece, it is called...

☐ Checkmate
✓ Stalemate
☐ Capture

→ Stalemate is one of several ways a game can end in a draw, because there is no possible escape.

#2 When one of your opponent's pieces occupies the same square as one of your pieces, it is a...

✓ Capture
☐ Check
☐ Checkmate

→ Capturing one of your opponent's pieces implies taking its place with one of yours and it is exactly the same when they capture one of your pieces.

Take a moment to remember how each piece moves and decide: is this check or checkmate?

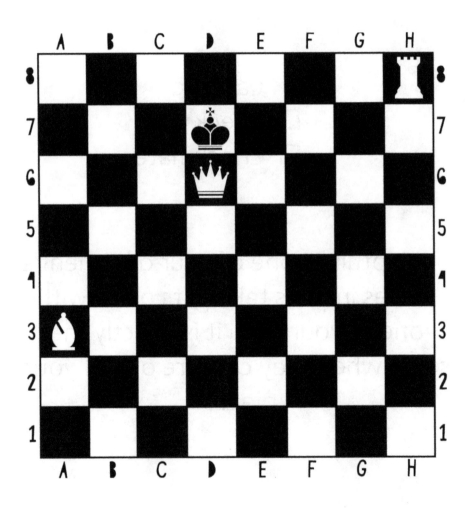

→ It's 'checkmate', but why? Let's look at all the moves that the black King can or cannot make.

If the black King moves to C8, D8, or E8, the white Rook can capture it on the next move.

If the black King moves to C6 or E6, the white Queen can also capture it on the next move.

And moving to D6 and capturing the white Queen makes the black King defenseless against the white Bishop.

You need to keep the King safe without moving it, what piece can help you?

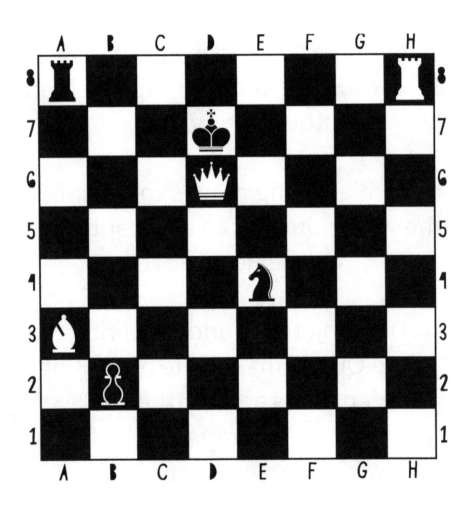

→ With these pieces, the only way of taking the black King out of check without moving it, is capturing the white Queen with the black Knight.

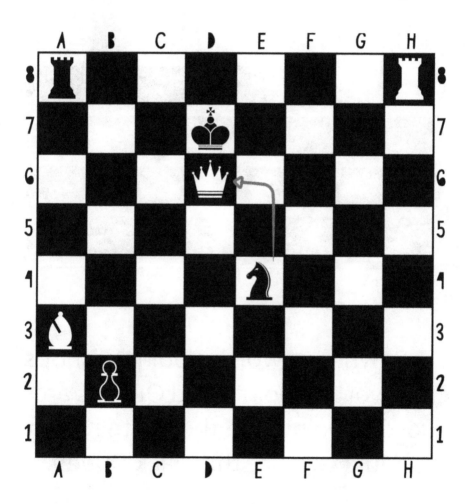

White pieces move: Taking into account each piece's value, which one should the white Knight capture?

→ Pawns are worth 1 point, Bishops are worth 3 points and Queens are worth 9 points - so the white Knight should capture the black Queen.

Black pieces move: The black King is under attack, where would you put it to avoid that threat?

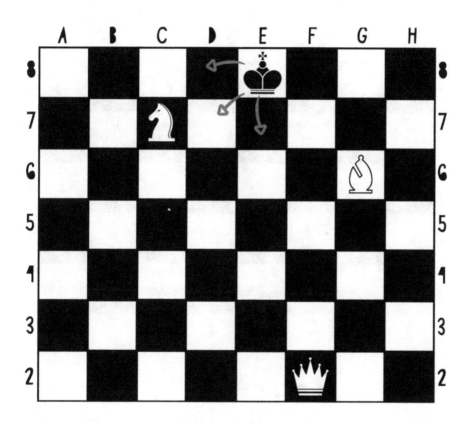

→ You can move the black King to any of these squares: D8, D7, or E7.

White pieces move: The white King is under attack, what would you do to protect it?

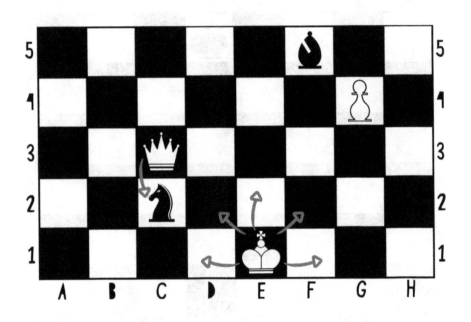

→ You can move the King to D1, D2, E2, F1, or F2. You could also capture the black Knight, but that would leave the white Queen defenseless.

Chapter 3: Special Moves

Choose the correct answer:

#1 When a Rook jumps over the King to protect it, it is called...

- ☐ Promotion
- ☐ En passant capture
- ✓ Castling

→ Castling is the only move that allows two pieces to move during the same turn and is also the only situation where a Rook can jump.

#2 When you capture one of your opponent's Pawns as it passes by one of your own Pawns, it is called...

- ☐ Promotion
- ✓ En passant capture
- ☐ Castling

→ Remember, an en passant capture is when a Pawn captures another Pawn that takes two steps on its first move as it passes by. It's easier to remember it knowing that 'en passant' in French for 'in passing'.

#3 When a Pawn moves far enough to reach the other side of the board, it gets promoted and can become a...

- ☐ Queen
- ☐ Rook
- ☐ Bishop
- ☐ Knight
- ✓ All of them

#4 Castling is a special move that can be made...

- ☐ Kingside
- ☐ Queenside
- ✓ Both

Look at these three steps, from top to bottom, and circle the special move you see:

En passant ⟨Castling⟩ Promotion

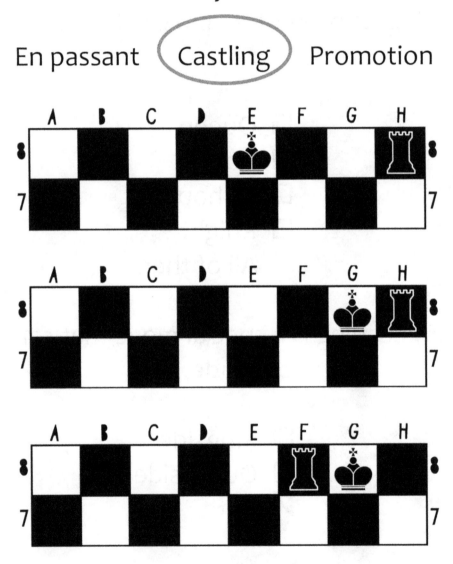

Look at these three steps, from left to right, and circle the special move you see:

En passant   Castling   Promotion

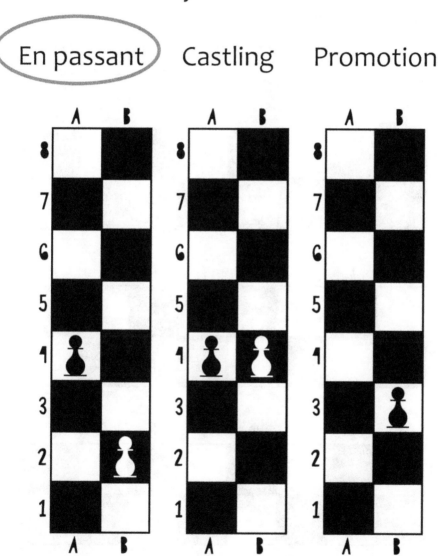

Look at these three steps, from top to bottom, and circle the special move you see:

En passant   Castling   (Promotion)

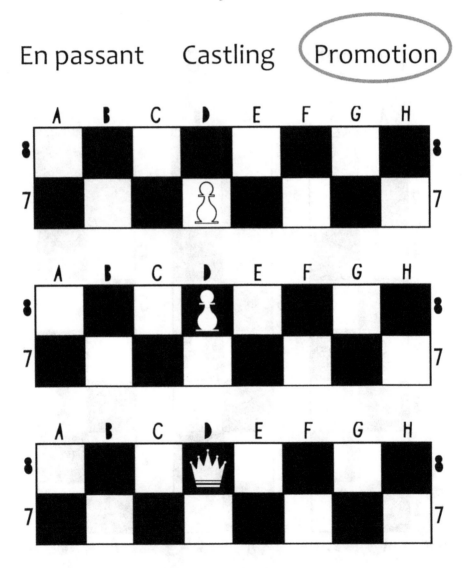

What piece would you promote your white Pawn to or which one would you move to put the black King in check?

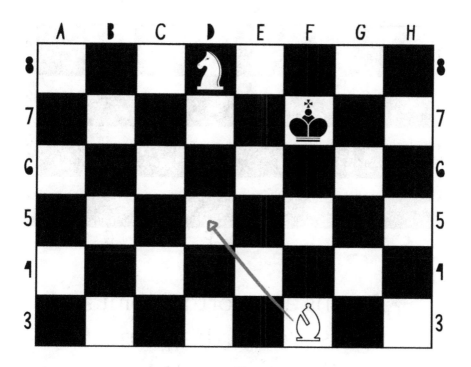

➤ You can move the white Bishop to D5 or promote the Pawn to a Knight.

The white Pawn on D4 just took two steps. Taking into account each piece's value, where would you place the black Pawn on C4?

→ Pawns are worth 1 point and Knights are worth 3 points, so moving the Pawn to B3 to capture the white Knight is a better option in this case.

Chapter 4: Basic Tactics

Choose the correct answer:

#1 If you attack a Queen that is shielding a Bishop, it is called...

- ✓ Relative skewer
- ☐ Relative pin
- ☐ Absolute skewer

→ Attacking a higher value piece that is shielding a lesser value one is called a skewer. Skewering any piece other than the King is a relative skewer.

#2 If you attack a Bishop that is shielding a King, it is called...

- ✓ Absolute pin
- ☐ Absolute skewer
- ☐ Relative pin

→ Remember, attacking a lesser value piece that is shielding a higher value piece is called a pin. If the piece being shielded is the King, it is called an absolute pin and you have to sacrifice the pinned piece because it is illegal to expose the King.

#3 If you prevent a Queen from advancing to another rank, but it can still move along that rank, it is called...

- ✓ Relative pin
- ☐ Partial pin
- ☐ Absolute pin

#4 If you attack a King and Queen at the same time with the same piece, it is called...

- ☐ Family fork
- ✓ Royal fork
- ☐ Grand fork

Can you find all 9 words related to the tactics in this Word search puzzle?

P	I	N	Y	F	O	R	K	T	G
A	B	O	M	J	G	T	S	D	R
R	R	E	L	A	T	I	V	E	A
T	K	E	U	R	O	Y	A	L	N
I	X	T	Z	E	A	N	P	A	D
A	B	S	O	L	U	T	E	W	P
L	I	F	A	M	I	L	Y	N	B
S	K	E	W	E	R	T	G	E	K

Choose a piece to fork the black King, Queen and Bishop at the same time:

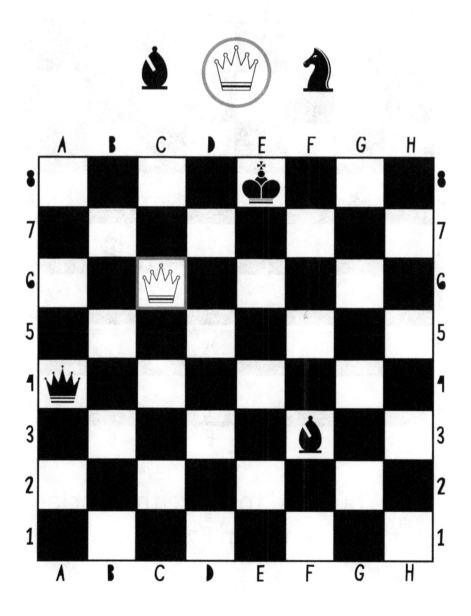

Black pieces move: What would you do to pin the white Knight and King?

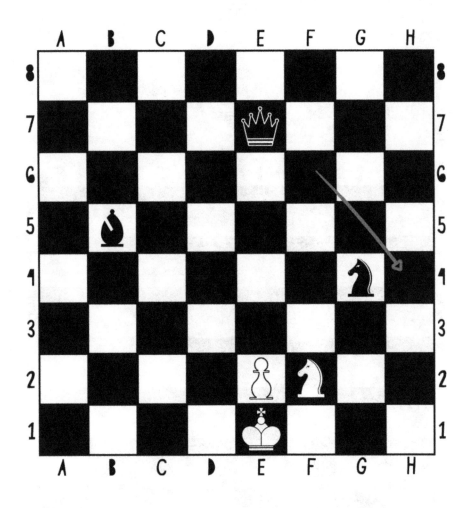

→ You need to move the black Queen from E7 to H4.

Black pieces move: What would you do to fork the white Pawn and Bishop?

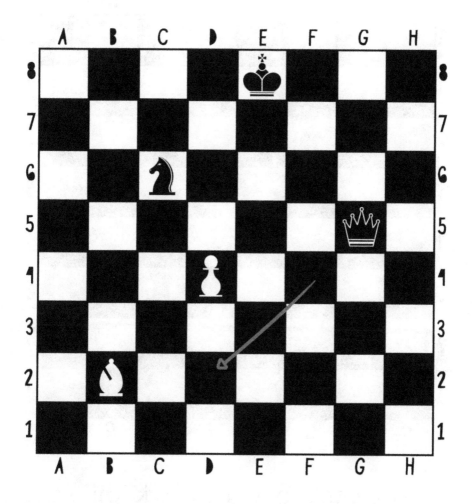

→ You need to move the black Queen from G5 to D2.

Black pieces move: What would you do to turn this skewer into a pin?

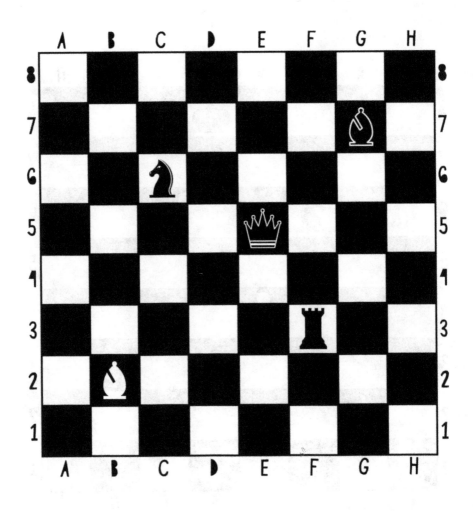

→ You can move the black Knight to D4 or the black Rook to C3.

Chapter 5: Opening Moves

Match each opening technique with the first piece that moves:

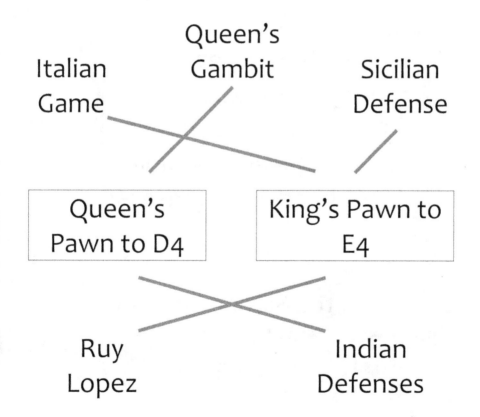

Italian Game

Queen's Gambit

Sicilian Defense

Queen's Pawn to D4

King's Pawn to E4

Ruy Lopez

Indian Defenses

In which opening techniques do the black pieces mirror the first move of the white pieces? That is, they move the black Queen's Pawn after the white one and the black King's Pawn after the white one.

- ✓ Ruy Lopez
- ✓ Italian Game
- ☐ Sicilian Defense
- ✓ Queen's Gambit
- ☐ Indian Defenses

→ In the Sicilian and Indian Defenses, the black pieces make a different move.

Black pieces move: What piece would you move to make this opening an Indian Defense?

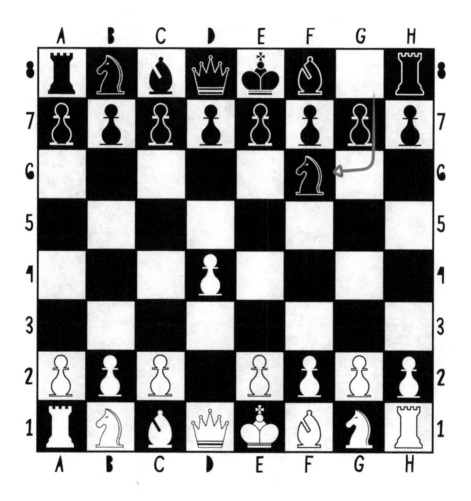

→ The black Knight from G8 to F6.

White pieces move: What piece would you move to make this opening a Queen's Gambit?

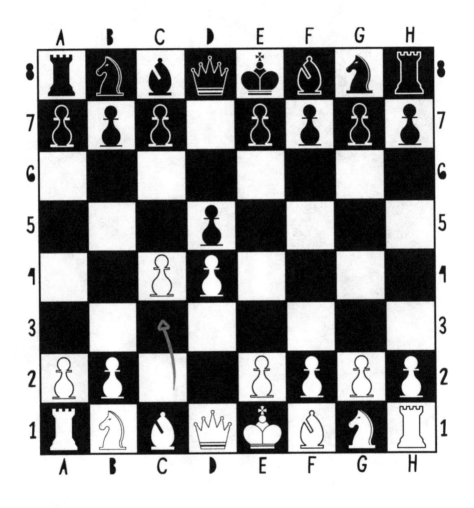

→ The white Pawn from C2 to C4.

White pieces move: Where would you place the Bishop on F1 to make this opening a Ruy Lopez?

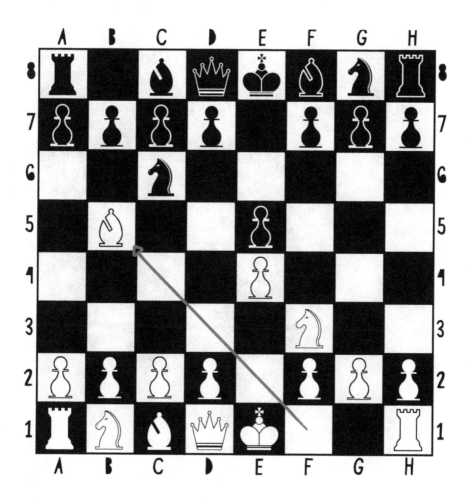

→ The white Bishop has to go on B5.

White pieces move: Where would you place the Bishop on F1 to make this opening an Italian Game?

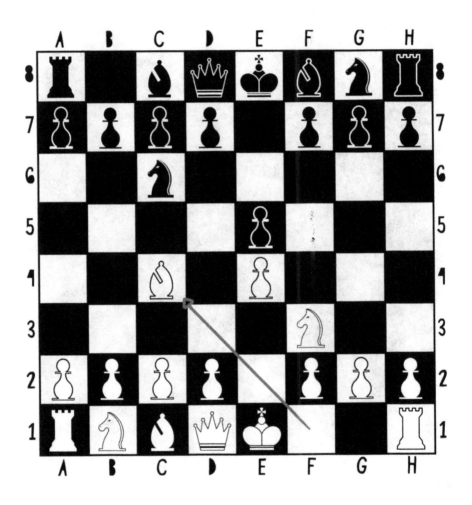

→ The white Bishop has to go on C4.

Chapter 6: Checkmates

Can you tell, without looking back, which checkmates you just learned?

- ☐ King and Queen
- ✓ Queen and Bishop
- ☐ Rook and Pawn
- ✓ Pawn and King
- ✓ Queen and Rook
- ☐ Knight and King
- ✓ Bishop and Knight
- ☐ King and Rook
- ✓ Queen and Knight

What piece needs to go on F5 to checkmate the black King?

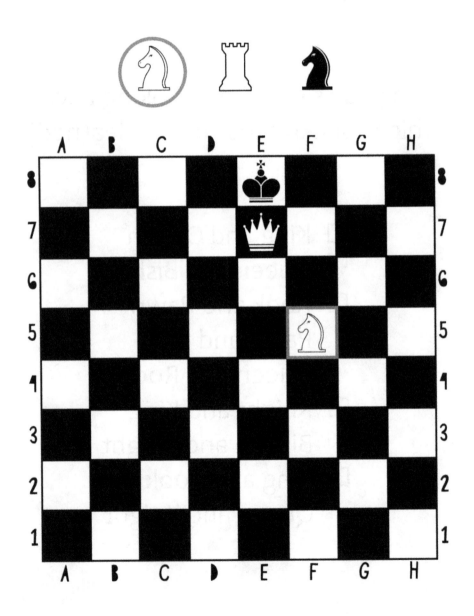

What piece needs to go on H1 to checkmate the white King?

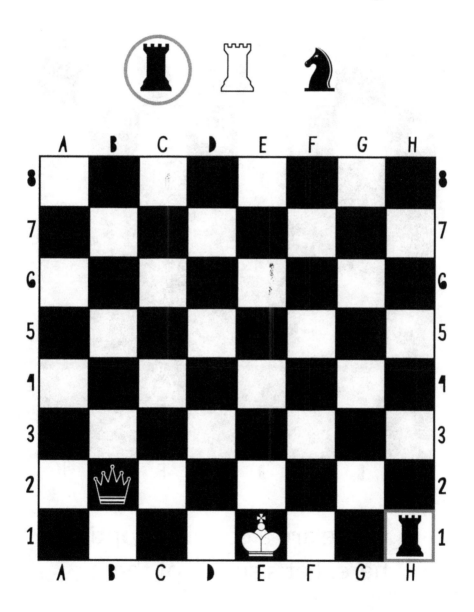

White pieces move: What would you do to checkmate the black King?

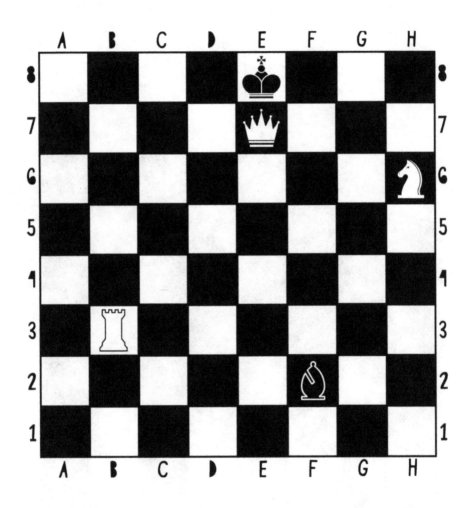

→ There are a couple of options here. Let's see all of them.

The white Queen is already preventing the black King from moving to D8, D7, F8, or F7, but it could capture the Queen to escape check.

To avoid that and checkmate the black King you can protect the Queen by:

#1 Moving the white Knight on H6 to G8 or F5.

#2 Moving the white Rook from B3 to B8.

Black pieces move: What would you do to checkmate the white King?

→ The black Rook has the white King already confined in the first rank. To checkmate it, just move the white Queen to C1.

White pieces move: What would you do to checkmate the black King?

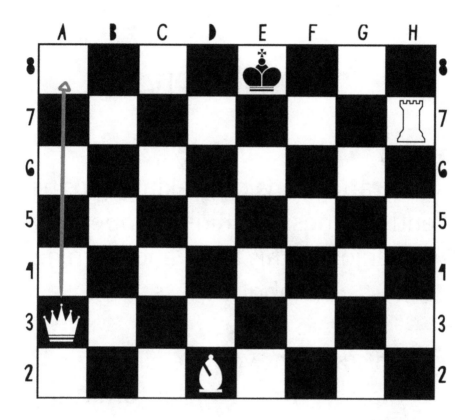

→ The white Rook has the black King trapped in the 8th rank, so you just need to move the white Queen to A8.

Conclusion

Congratulations on making it to the end of 'Chess for Kids'! I hope that you enjoyed this book and learning all about chess.

I'm sure that you are already a master. Now it's your turn to practice as much as you want and challenge your friends and family.

Have a great time!

If you found this book useful, a positive review on Amazon is always appreciated!

Bye!

CPSIA information can be obtained
at www.ICGtesting.com
Printed in the USA
BVHW042347170322
631771BV00017B/1591

9 781922 805010